MORE
Things
They
Didn't
Teach Me
in
Worship Leading
School

Compiled and edited by

TOM KRAEUTER

Emerald Books
P.O. Box 635
Lynnwood, Washington 98046

Training Resources • Hillsboro Missouri

More Things They Didn't Teach Me in Worship Leading School
        © 1998 Training Resources, Inc.
        8929 Old LeMay Ferry Road
        Hillsboro, MO 63050
        (314) 789-4522

ISBN 1-883002-67-2

Published by Emerald Books
P.O. Box 635
Lynnwood WA 98046

Printed in the U.S.A.

Dedication

We, the writers of this book, humbly dedicate these stories of our experiences to the thousands of men and women around the world who regularly lead worship in a local church. Thank you for your dedicated "front-lines" ministry. We pray that you will glean both comfort and wisdom from our experiences.

Thanks to

The many people who got the original book (*Things They Didn't Teach Me in Worship Leading School*) and were inspired and encouraged enough by it to suggest we do a sequel.

Those who have prayed for the completion of this book (no small task since it was over two years in the making!).

Jennifer Brody for great editing (and re-editing) that helped make even the best worship leaders sound like writers.

My family for the patience and time it took to make this book a reality...thanks!

Contents

Steve Bowersox

Steve Bowersox is the founder and president of the Bowersox Institute of Music, a nonprofit organization dedicated to the development of the musician in worship. He is the founding executive director of Integrity Music's Worship International and currently serves as music director.

Steve holds several degrees in music and business and has authored the "Worship Musician's Theory Course," "Vocal Aerobics: A Fitness Program for Your Voice," "'MIDI'anites Redeemed" and the "Worship Leaders Survival Kit." He has toured with several prominent musicians and is proficient in wind instruments, guitar, bass, electronic keyboard and MIDI.

Steve is recognized as one of the pioneers and leaders for technology in the Church. His humor, mixed with excellent inspirational teaching ministers to the spirit, refreshes the mind and motivates believers to stir up their gifts. Steve travels around the world teaching on worship as a lifestyle, leadership, and musical excellence.

Steve, his wife, Rebecca, and their daughter, Rachel, live in Jacksonville, Florida.

The Piano Lesson

Pastor asked me if I was available after the morning service for lunch. Being a bachelor at the time, and considering my options, I was more than happy to accommodate. As I began to inquire, I found out we were going to a member's home to look at and listen to a grand piano we might acquire for our sanctuary. Now I was really excited. A home cooked meal and a new grand piano! I liked the upright we had from our old building, but it just didn't fit the decor or style of our new sanctuary.

As we walked into the living room, I saw a gorgeous piano shining in the front sitting area. The room looked as if it had been built for the piano. As we exchanged greetings, the piano almost sparkled in the sunlight. The dark lines in the grain of the brown mahogany were a perfect accent to the room. The finish was so shiny and smooth it could have been used to do a commercial for furniture polish! Our hostess was in a difficult place financially and this beautiful piano, which had been financed, was creating a real problem for her. Our church was considering the purchase of this piano to help her out and to obtain a much needed grand piano for ourselves.

Everyone was excited and asked me to play. The truth is I don't think I'd ever seen a piano that was as nice a piece of furniture. As I lifted the lid covering the keys, I saw a name I didn't recognize, but even the lettering was quality. I guess I didn't know as much about pianos as I thought. After all, the conservatory only had two types of pianos: Steinways and Yamahas. I knew a few other brands but, not many.

The moment of truth arrived. I was already dreaming of the melodies and harmonic lines I would play. "I'll start with something everyone knows and let this baby really sing," I thought. I ran off an arpeggio to introduce a beautiful song. Ugh! I could hardly push the keys down. It was like moving wet cement! The sound was okay—a little mushy, I thought—but what was wrong with the action? Everyone else smiled and oooed and aahed over it. I was ready to soak my hands, and I hadn't even played one refrain! I kindly asked our hostess if she played very often. She replied she really couldn't play, but that she had always wanted a grand piano. It was actually more for show than sound. Hmm, I guess so. Well, maybe it just needed to be broken in, or maybe I had gotten soft on that old upright.

Lunch was being served. I played a bit longer as everyone was seated. It was a little out of tune—no matter, that could be fixed. I was running scales, playing songs I knew, showing off my best music store licks! But, oh, was the action stiff. Was there something inside holding the keys down? No, just standard piano hammers. I finally joined the others at the table, and it seemed like someone dropped a cue and everyone looked at me and asked,

"What do you think of the piano?" Uh, oh! I hadn't even eaten yet!

I answered as nicely and honestly as I could. "Uh, well, it is a beautiful piano, but it is very hard to play. The key action is really stiff and it was a real workout to play." Someone said, "Yeah, well, it's a new piano. It should loosen up after you bang on it a while!" We all kind of laughed and went on with the meal. Afterwards, I went back to the piano to play it again. Maybe it had improved! The pastor walked in and looked at my forlorn scowl. "Steve, we really need to help her out here. She could lose everything because of the way this thing is financed." I said, "Oh, please don't buy this—I can't play this thing. It's a beautiful piece of furniture, but it is not a musical instrument. If we have to, let's buy it and give it to the Methodist Church down the street!" I guess that sounded funnier than I had intended, because that got a real chuckle from the pastor. He then said something that pierced my heart and I knew it was right from the heart of God. "Steve, the most important thing in ministry is people—our people, any hurting people. In the scope of God's master plan this piano is really not that significant... but her life is!"

I let out a sigh. "Yeah, you're right," I said, "but this will be my instrument of worship. I will have to lead the people into the presence of God, and battle this thing the whole way! Maybe it will get better, I'll get a technician out to work on it." The deal was done.

The next Sunday the new grand piano was in the sanctuary. It did look great on stage. Everyone in the congregation was excited to hear this new piano. So we took off with a "greatest hits" list of worship songs. About half way through the list, my hands were exhausted. My fingers felt bruised, I had broken almost every finger nail. And, to make matters worse, the lady we had bought this piano from was on the front row, just grinning from ear to ear! Everyone was in a great place of worship—except me! I was angry! I was hurting! I knew this would happen! I told them! I began to despise this piano.

Well, this is pretty much how it went for over two years. I had a couple different technicians look at that piano several times—and it improved slightly. Eventually, the keys began sticking after I played them. They would just stay down! I would push them down, then lift them up again to push them down again. A couple of times the sustain pedal bar just fell off the piano. I'd do one of those a capella worship things so I could crawl underneath the piano and hook it back up! Not only that, but the piano would go out of tune during a service. You could hear it drop in pitch! I would have brought out the old upright, but someone had given it to the Methodist Church down the road! (Where did they get that idea from anyway?!)

Despite the piano, our church continued in explosive growth. Our worship really intensified, and we had many awesome times in the presence of the Lord. The lady that had originally owned the piano joined the choir and became an outstanding alto soloist. As Pastor foresaw, she got back on her feet and was a substantial member.

From that church, I left to start a worship training ministry called "Worship International" with Integrity Music. It was difficult leaving my church family and friends, but we all knew this was of the Lord. Sometime after I left, the church purchased a new piano! One of those nice electronic grands by Roland! Mmm, it was nice—and always in tune!

One day I asked the Lord why I had to deal with that Old Bang-n-Chang piano. He told me I could have been delivered sooner if I hadn't struck the rock that God used to help His people get free in worship! Wow! I immediately saw how I had acted like Moses and struck the rock. In Numbers 20:8, God instructed Moses to speak to the rock before the eyes of the people, and the rock will pour out water. The entire community would live from this. But, when Moses faced the people, he was irritated by their rebellion. He said, "Listen you rebels, must we bring you water out of this rock?" Moses struck the rock, not once, but twice with his rod. God still performed the miracle, yet Moses had sinned with his anger and his pride. I also think it's interesting to note that he struck the rock with his rod, which symbolizes a work of the hand or individual strength. God had instructed him to speak to the rock, something of the breath which symbolizes the Spirit. In verse 12, God says, "Because you did not trust in me enough to honor me as holy in the sight of the Israelites, you will not bring this community into the land I give them." God was still honoring His promise to the people, but Moses would not enter the Promised Land.

Neither one of us entered our Promised Land! For me the Promised Land would have been at least a new Roland keyboard. Oftentimes, we see the short current affliction and focus on that instead of the blessings and growth. Or we start to depend upon our own talents and strength instead of keeping our trust in the Lord.

I like God's sense of humor in my situation. He told me I could have been delivered sooner if I hadn't struck the rock. Even *He* called that piano a rock! The whole experience was one of growing and learning for me. I would never trade those days of worship. It was really the place and time for me to cut my teeth as a worship leader. I know the anointing of the Lord grew on me in those days, despite my attitude toward the piano. Praise God for His mercy. And I'm grateful to see the growth of the former piano owner. She really did come a long way in the things of the Lord. She even became a special friend to me. Pastor was right—people are the most important thing in ministry. God is more interested in tuning lives than instruments.

Such a valuable lesson to learn—and besides, I have really strong hands now!!

Phil Christensen

Phil Christensen is a worship pastor and veteran Christian musician from the Pacific Northwest, best known for his writing in Worship Leader magazine and CCM.

For years, Phil has been researching and documenting the stories behind our favorite praise songs. His "Song Stories" is a regular feature of Worship Leader. He is currently finishing his first book of these stories for Kregel Publications.

Phil has also opened "Indie Central," a place where hundreds of independent worship artists network and submit their praise projects for possible review in Worship Leader magazine.

An alumnus of Multnomah Bible College, he has been the worship pastor of Church on the Mountain near Mt. Hood, Oregon for many years. Phil enjoys writing, music and mountain biking.

Phil, his wife, Mitzi, and their four children, Philip, Stefan, Dylan and Megan, live an hour east of Portland in the Hoodland Corridor.

Andy Walks with Me

———⬤————

"Seriously bad worship" would have been an understatement.

First, I was leading a song I loathed. It was a silly 20th century gospel piece called "In the Garden," that included lines like, "and the voice I hear, falling on my ear..."

The band dragged lamely through the dated little waltz and never lifted their eyes from the chord charts. The vocal team hovered on the brink of giggles as they choked out, "...and He walks with me, and He talks with me." The congregation, looking like bored junior high students, stared blankly at their tattered red hymnals. At least Pastor Mike managed to salvage the wasted time; he reviewed his sermon notes.

And as if our journey to the Throne wasn't *already* a trainwreck, the worship service was about to get much worse.

In the fourth row, an apparently drunk visitor began to bellow out "In the Garden" as if it were a German drinking song. His thundering voice was a cross between Gilbert Gottfried and Jerry Lewis.

He repeatedly shouted, "You guys are great! I love this!" and "This is for me!" He danced and jumped from the floor to the pew.

Yes, this was seriously bad worship, and I was eager to end it. We closed the set with a simple version of "Jesus Loves Me," but that seemed to *really* set off our visitor.

He flailed about wildly, bawling out the lyrics as if he were the only person in the world. In a way, he was; everyone else in the auditorium had stopped singing and now watched me in amusement to see what I would do.

I've had root canals that were more fun.

This little nightmare had actually started about three weeks before, when the Lord made it clear that I should lead "In the Garden." While He didn't send me an e-mail or a Candy-gram, it was obvious enough—even a dense worship leader like myself couldn't miss *That* Voice.

Had He assigned me a new Maranatha or Hosanna piece, I would have obeyed Him in a heartbeat, but "In the Garden"? I'd been reading the right books and learning the right songs, and "In the Garden" didn't fit anywhere. It was neither contemporary nor classic. It was simply bad poetry set to an even worse waltz. Lyrics like, "and He bids me go, through the voice of woe," were unfathomably awful, but no worse than the melody and chord structure.

I dismissed the prompting of the Holy Spirit and went about my business.

The following week, my wife, Mitzi, received a lovely centerpiece as a gift. It was a dried floral arrangement set on an opened, gilded hymnal, a book permanently opened to... you guessed it: "In The Garden." I walked past the reminder every time I entered the living room, but still balked and refused to lower myself to what I considered sappy, religious fluff.

It had now been three weeks, and the Holy Spirit would not leave me alone. Strangers at the grocery store were whistling "In the Garden." Randomly, several people volunteered to me that it was their favorite song. Every Scripture I read seemed to mention gardens. Mitzi told me she wanted to start a garden.

Half-heartedly, I obeyed God. I condescendingly brought "In the Garden" to rehearsal, and we gave a valiant effort to spark up the little song. While we had developed a few skills at giving hymns a loving face-lift, "In The Garden" was hopeless.

The song was pure corn, but God had pulled rank on me.

Our song line-up that week also included a simple version of "Jesus Loves Me" and a story to introduce it.

The worship-set was now over, though, and our wild man was still clapping and whistling for more. It would have been no surprise if he had held up a lighter and thrown Frisbees. I put my guitar in its stand, slipped off my headset microphone, and slunk from the platform into the fellowship hall.

Glenda, a terrific lady, was waiting for me there. "I am so sorry, Phil," she was saying. "That noisy man came with my son Brady."

"It's no big deal," I mumbled politely, but I really wanted to massage my mangled ego and cradle a hot cup of coffee.

"I need to tell you something," she insisted, and her words began to jolt me quicker than any caffeine.

Glenda explained that the young man's name was Andy. He had been in a mental institution his *entire life*. Brady rehabilitates men like Andy and had spent the past two years trying to get him ready to face the outside world. This trek to our church had represented the First Big Excursion into life for Andy.

My heart softened a bit as I heard this, but I was about to be changed forever by the next revelation.

Andy's therapy had included singing, and Brady took two years patiently teaching him two songs...

...I heard it coming even before Glenda said it.

Andy's two songs were "In The Garden" and "Jesus Loves Me."

Glenda thanked me for being sensitive to the Holy Spirit, apologized again for Andy's interruptions and returned to her seat. She was tearful and clearly moved by what God had done.

I began to weep too, but mine were tears of shame and repentance. It was obvious that God had arranged this event specifically for Andy. While I had asked the Lord many times to work *through* me, today He had worked *in spite of* me. The True Worship Leader had even factored my arrogance and pride into His planning.

"This is for me!" Andy had cried joyfully about that precious time of worship. And clearly, in so many beautiful ways, it was.

But God had planted a message for all of us "In the Garden" that morning. A message of tenderness. A message of pursuit. A message of measureless love.

After worship was over, Andy returned to his simple dorm room. He was filled with childlike confidence and delight in the fact that God had orchestrated those songs especially for him.

Glenda and Brady drove home knowing they had just witnessed a miracle.

And I, a worship leader who *should* have known better, walked away with a dramatic new understanding of how intimately God cherishes His people and their praises. For a fleeting moment I grasped the truth that the King Eternal who steers the stars with flawless precision is equally determined to move heaven and earth—and even the hearts of stubborn worship pastors—to meet and embrace His children.

For He truly is the God who whispers in our ears with a voice like none other—the One who walks with us, talks with us, and tells us in ways more wonderful than we ever could imagine—that we are, in fact, His very own.

Randy Rothwell

Randy Rothwell has been using music and song to magnify the Lord since 1972. He is committed to a lifestyle of wholehearted worship and to helping others discover the same. Saved at the early age of 14, Randy soon discovered that his love for music could be used as a powerful tool through which God's great love and power would flow and draw others closer to Jesus.

Randy has been the worship leader on five of Integrity's Hosanna! Music recordings including "Mighty Warrior," "Army of God," "Worship the King," "Be Magnified" as well as "The Best of Randy Rothwell: Remembering His Goodness." He has also been involved in creating new products designed specifically as tools to benefit smaller churches, home groups and family worship times, entitled "Praise and Worship for Small Groups."

Randy is currently traveling full-time, ministering in local churches, seminars, conferences, worship retreats and Christian music festivals, with a burning desire to see every part of the Body of Christ come into a deeper experience and knowledge of the presence of the Lord in praise and worship.

Randy, his wife, Dana, and their daughter, Melody, make their home in Franklin, Tennessee.

Breaking the Sound Barrier

One of the major things that can affect the experience of corporate worship is the quality of sound you hear. A full, rich and balanced mix can make a big difference. I personally love an excellent P.A. system, and nothing thrills me more than great sounding monitors. To hear my guitar sounding clean and crisp and to hear my voice sounding clear and strong helps me to feel more confident and, quite frankly, more in control. However, more times than I can count, the Lord has used a sound system to help me understand that it is He Who is in control of the worship, not me.

Often I find myself leading worship in various churches, conferences and seminars where the sound system is much less than desirable. Or perhaps even worse, the P.A. system may be excellent, but the person operating the sound system has no "ear" for music and has—to be kind—no earthly idea what they are doing. This can prove to be quite a distraction for me if I allow it to be.

Sometimes when I arrive at a church and assess the P.A. system, my heart sinks. I begin to think that the worship time is not going to be what it could be because of the sound quality. This has frequently caused me to have the attitude of not giving my best to the people in the meeting. It has taken me a long time to finally realize that the what people really desire is to experience the Lord's presence in a fresh and powerful way and to leave the gathering feeling that we have been unified and drawn closer to God.

I remember a particular event that happened when I was a teenager and a brand new Christian, back in the early 70's. In my hometown of Paducah, Kentucky, the church that I attended was made up of mostly teenagers, like myself, who were newly saved and excited about Jesus Christ.

One night when we came to church the late Keith Green, a very popular Christian musician at the time, was there. Our pastor had heard that he was touring in the Southeast and had somehow persuaded him to make an appearance at our small gathering. You can imagine the excitement of having such a nationally-known Christian artist come to our small town. Needless to say this was not a normal performance stop for him. The crowd was much smaller. The building was smaller. I imagine the honorarium was much smaller. Of course, the sound system was much, much less than that to which he was accustomed. In fact, we had the old Shure Vocal Master column speakers (I affectionately referred to it as the Shure Vocal Smasher!).

Well, Keith came in and got the best sound he could out of the P.A. and then just went on. I was struck by his confidence, his complete abandonment to God and his joy in the presence of the Lord. He didn't just sing and entertain; he really worshiped. I felt united with him and all my brothers and sisters as we worshiped the Lord together. It was a very special time.

How different that night would have been if Keith had allowed himself to be distracted and annoyed by the limitations of our sound system.

I think about this in relation to my own worship leading experiences. After I have rehearsed and gotten the best sound check I possibly can, I simply need to go forward and stay focused on the Lord, no matter what the natural circumstances may be. I have learned that the majority of folks in the congregation are totally oblivious to most of the little things that I find distracting and annoying. I must stay focused and trust God to minister to each heart. After all, He is God. (Duh?!) We need to give up our right to be in control and allow the grace and power of God to take over.

Darrell Evans

Darrell Evans began his walk with Christ when he was only 11 years old. Shortly thereafter, he began writing songs and leading other youth in worship. Eventually, following evangelism and ministry training, Evans served as youth pastor and worship leader for churches in California, Washington, and Oklahoma.

Darrell's albums include the Hosanna! Music recording, "Let the River Flow" and Vertical Music recordings "You Are I Am" and "Freedom." His songs include "Let the River Flow," "We Will Embrace (Your Move)" and "My God Reigns."

When Darrell was a kid he wanted to be a comedian. In fact he does a pretty impressive Jerry Lewis imitation.

Darrell and his wife, Gayla, reside in Mobile, Alabama. From Mobile, the couple head River Flow Ministries, a full-time worship concert ministry that is carrying them into churches across the U.S.

The Playground of Praise

One of my favorite things to do is to take long walks and spend time in worship and prayer. Some of the most significant exchanges between the Lord and me occur while I am on these walks. Sometimes I listen to a worship tape in my walkman, sometimes I simply walk and talk with the Lord, and some days I just quiet my heart and listen. Often, worship songs are birthed out of these prayer walks.

About three years ago I was out on a walk with the Lord through my neighborhood heading toward a nearby elementary school yard. I was listening to a demo recording of a new song that I was writing, "We'll dance and we'll sing for our God is the Ancient of Days." I felt the Father tugging at my heart saying, "I want you to dance for Me. I want you to dance with Me." I stopped the tape. Still, I kept hearing, "Will you dance for Me." It was as though the Holy Spirit was saying, "You said you would in the song. Now, will you dance for me out here on this field?"

At this point in my life I had been a worship leader for several years. Although I believed that dancing before the Lord was a biblical expression of praise, it was not an expression in which I felt freedom. I particularly enjoyed the quiet love songs and intimate times with the Lord.

Anytime in my life when there had been an opportunity to dance before the Lord, I usually felt as though the worship leader was trying to hype it up or manipulate me into that expression. The truth is that I simply used that as an excuse.

So here the Lord was asking me to go for it out on a football field. On one side was a line of neighborhood houses with their backyards facing me, and on the other side was the school playground where the kids were playing at recess. I had an opportunity to let the Lord release in me a childlike heart of worship.

After a few moments of indecision I turned the music on again. I thought, "Okay, here we go." I started at one end of the field and began dancing and spinning my way toward the other end. About halfway down the field, I began shouting (another valid biblical expression of worship that was always difficult for me) at the top of my lungs, "Hey, hey, hey, freedom!" Over and over again I yelled and spun around and danced before the Lord. It was great! I didn't care who might see or hear me.

I had known the reverence of an awesome God and the intimacy of a loving Jesus. However, at that moment I was truly understanding the joy of a totally abandoned childlike heart. I was celebrating with my Father on this playground that I was His son. Something in me had cracked and peeled. A layer of pride had been pulled away. I had a new sense of freedom. This freedom translated into leading others into the same abandonment in worship.

I believe that our personalities can affect our inter-action with the Lord. However, this should never be used as an excuse to give God anything less than what Scrip-ture calls for as passionate and creative expressions of worship to the Lord. "That's not my personality," doesn't work with the Lord. The very nature of worship is to step beyond ourselves and recognize that He is greater and we are less. He is our Father and we are His kids.

Is there one thing that you said you would never do in worship? Is there one expression you could never see yourself helping others experience? Do that! The result will be new levels of freedom in your life and in the lives of those you humbly intend to serve.

Beth Emery-Bryant

Beth Emery-Bryant, an ordained minister, demonstrates an excellent combination of anointing and musical ability in ministry. Used of the Lord as a speaker, teacher, worship leader, musician, soloist, choir and orchestra director, etc., Beth has ministered throughout the nations in conferences and churches. Her travels and 22 years of experience in local church ministry have given Beth valuable insights and spiritual wisdom making her a faithful servant to the Body of Christ.

Beth is a gifted worship leader with a heart after God. Her desire is to see the body enter more fully into the presence of the Lord with full expression of worship. This, she believes, is the key to victorious Christian living. Her two worship manuals, "Reconstructing Your Worship Ministry" and "Worship Leaders Handbook" are excellent tools for church ministry. Beth has also released two of her own recordings, "Glorious Worship" and "Come Up Higher."

Beth and her husband, Vincent, live in Maryland near Washington, D.C.

Holy Spirit Piano Lessons

It was the eleventh hour. Holding my ten fingers up I cried out to God, quoting a desperate prayer, "Lord, teach my fingers to fight and my hands to do warfare... Father, in the name of Jesus, anoint my fingers to play the piano for Your glory and honor (Psalm 144:1). You have gifted and anointed my voice to sing and lead people to You in worship. Thank You for touching my life and giving me the ability to sing Your praises. Lord, I ask You to give me the same ability to play the piano. Anoint my fingers with ten times the power. Amen."

Four months earlier, coming on staff of this large congregation had been an answer to prayer. I was serving as the minister of music and youth. I felt as though I was in the middle of God's will. The church was Spirit-led and expressive in their worship. Sunday morning praise and worship would flow in concert with the Holy Spirit and was enhanced by the skill and sensitivity of our pianist, Carol. I had depended greatly on her skill. Now Carol, our wonderful pianist, was transferring to another state and there was a slight problem: who would take her place? No one else seemed to be available. I certainly was not capable. A degree in music majoring in vocal pedagogy and ten years of experience of serving on church staffs had made my pastor feel that I, as minister of music, should be able to handle every area of the music department. Although I had the credentials, my skill level at the keyboard was *very* limited, certainly not at the necessary level to accompany choirs or the worship service.

So, here I was, after ten years of full-time ministry, in a quandary because I couldn't play the piano. One thing I have learned about God is that when He calls someone into ministry, regardless of age, He uses every-thing—giftings, experiences, knowledge—to prepare that person for leadership.

He called me when I was five years old, and I knew with certainty from that time that He was going to use me in ministry someday. I can look back over my life and see how He had groomed and prepared me for this very mo-ment. As a young child every time I saw someone play the piano, I coveted the gift and found myself drawn to that instrument. I longed to take piano lessons but never was afforded the opportunity. Even when I was in college my lack of skill at the keyboard caused me to dread taking the piano proficiency exam. However, the exam was a gradua-tion requirement for music majors. After four years of try-ing, I did finally pass the proficiency exam...but only by the grace of God and my sympathetic music professors.

Not being able to play the piano had been a handi-cap throughout my life as a music minister. The church had hired me as their chief musician, and they expected me to come through for them on the piano or find a replacement. In two weeks Carol would leave! With no one available in the congregation, I consulted the yellow pages. I spent several days on the phone, calling every music store and recording studio in the area. I ran down every lead. Each one turned out to be a dead end. For the first time in my music career I felt really desperate.

Finally, after two weeks of scheming (not to mention a huge telephone bill) I surrendered in defeat. Reaching for my Bible, I sighed in anguish, "Lord, I can't believe there is no one to help me..." My Bible opened to Psalm 144 and I read the first two verses, "Praise be to the LORD my Rock, who trains my hands for war, my fingers for battle. He is my loving God and my fortress, my stronghold and my deliverer, my shield, in whom I take refuge..." (Psalm 144:1-2). As I read the words of David, faith welled up in my heart. I prayed for God to do for me what He had done for David, to teach my fingers to fight and my hands to do warfare.

Walking over to the piano with my hands lifted to the Lord, I sat down. As I placed my fingers to strike a chord, it was as though the Holy Spirit Himself was guiding me. "Drop your middle finger and you have a minor chord. Pull your thumb down a half-step and you have a major seventh chord; pull your thumb down a whole step and you have a seventh chord. Move your little finger up a half a step and you have an augmented chord." Suddenly everything I had learned in years of studying music theory was transferred from my head to my fingers! I started to arpeggiate chords across the keyboard. This was beyond my capabilities. I knew it was a divine supernatural encounter with the Holy Spirit. Struck with awe over what was happening before my eyes, I was afraid to breathe for fear of losing this new gift. Excitement was rising within me, when I looked at the music I could actually play and sing at the same time!

This miracle happened so suddenly I began to cry. It was obvious that God had come through for me at the last hour. Tomorrow was Carol's last Sunday with our church and all of my scheming in my own strength had come to nothing. But the Lord's mighty power is inexhaustible!

I continued to play through the night, as the prompting of the Holy Spirit continued. My fingers ached but it was an exhilarating experience. I did not want to stop playing.

The next morning during the worship service, Carol was asked to leave the piano to join her husband on the platform for prayer. The congregation was sending them off with blessings. As the music ended I slipped in next to her and continued playing where she left off. Listening to the audio tape of that service, the point where she stopped playing and I started is indiscernible. No one in the congregation realized what an awesome moment that was.

For the duration of ministry at that church, I continued playing the piano. I even began giving piano lessons to church members! This precious miracle happened over eleven years ago. Since then, I have traveled around the world playing the piano and leading worship, knowing God truly has sent me this ability as a gift to use for His glory.

The key is discovering His power buried within each of us. In the time of His choosing, it is His power that enables us to be everything He desires. "Now to Him who is able to do immeasurably more than all we ask or imagine, according to His *power* that is at work within us, to Him be glory in the church and in Christ Jesus throughout all generations..." (Ephesians 3:20-21).

Each of us has a least one talent. If we do not bury or try to hide it, the Lord will multiply our talents to bring glory to Himself. David, the little shepherd boy, sat out on the back side of the desert playing his harp before the Lord and the stars of heaven. He was *discovering* and *developing* his gift. Then God added anointing to his skill. Later, in the presence of King Saul, God could *depend* upon David to play skillfully, driving away a demonic heaviness that was oppressing Saul. *Discover* your talent and *develop* it. Then *depend* on God to use you.

God used King David. He uses me. He can use you.

May the glory of the Lord cover the earth as we continue to worship Him in spirit and in truth!

Robb Redman

Dr. Robb Redman is an author, teacher and speaker. An ordained pastor in the Presbyterian Church (USA), Robb has a bachelor's degree from New College, University of Edinburgh, Scotland, and a doctorate in theology from the University of Erlangen, Germany.

Prior to his doctoral study, he served as pastor of the Brookings Presbyterian Church in Brookings, Oregon. He was associate professor of theology and ministry as well as director of the doctor of ministry program at Fuller Theological Seminary from 1991-1997. During this time he also directed worship ministry training at Maranatha! Music. Robb has authored a book, "Reformulating Reformed Theology" (University Press of America, 1997), and several reviews and articles, and serves as an editorial consultant for Worship Leader *magazine.*

Robb lives in San Antonio, Texas, with his wife, Pam. They have a St. Bernard named Clara, and enjoy cooking, movies, reading and exploring the Texas hill country.

A Pastor's Part in Worship

⟨⫘⟩

As a rookie pastor, I learned a lot of lessons on the job for which seminary could not have prepared me. That's not the fault of the seminary. After all, how could they account for everything churches can throw at a greenhorn?

I cut my teeth as a worship leader strumming my guitar for the InterVarsity group at my college. Those were powerful times of praise and community. I don't know why, but I think I expected my first church to be like that group. As I result, I learned the hard way what's most important about introducing contemporary worship music to a traditional church.

In 1985, after just about a year on the job, I spent my two-week study leave at Fuller Seminary in Pasadena. One Sunday evening I visited the Anaheim Vineyard with Professor Eddie Gibbs. The worship music of the Vineyard was entirely new to me and very liberating. I bought all their tapes and sheet music. For the next several weeks I listened to the tapes and practiced. After discussing it with the session (the governing board of elders in Presbyterian church) we agreed to replace the opening hymn with new songs.

We took a big risk. When the organist finished the prelude, I put my guitar on over my Presbyterian pastor's robes and stepped up to the microphone. I looked goofy, but I didn't care. I was so enthusiastic about these songs and the authenticity of worship they released in me. I described how I discovered them and my desire to lead the church in singing a new song to the Lord. I taught the people by singing through the song once, and then invited the congregation to join in. The response was positive. The 11:00 service went well, too, though not quite as enthusiastic.

Afterward, the elders encouraged me to keep the songs in the early service, which had a more informal atmosphere, but they thought the songs didn't belong in the later service. We were set. Long before people knew what to call it, we had a "blended" worship service. Soon a woman in the church began to sing and play guitar with me. We continued until I left the church to pursue doctoral studies at the end of 1986. People appreciated the fresh, personal approach of the music and the way they counterbalanced the depth of classic Presbyterian psalms and hymns. My last service in that church was a Christmas service led by a full band.

What did I learn in the process? First, I learned the importance of my role in modeling worship for the congregation and giving people permission to worship. I didn't fully understand that back then. I believed in prayerful planning, but I generally thought of my role in the service as a preacher and liturgist. To me, the choir and organist were the song leaders. I discovered that pastoral leadership can't be delegated. As goofy as I looked with my robes and guitar, it sent an unmistakable signal to the church: I was assuming responsibility for leading the praise of the people. There is no substitute for pastoral leadership in worship.

The other major lesson I learned is that the authenticity of worship did not depend on my performance. I was not a very good guitarist or singer, but the congregation, particularly at the early service, did not respond to my musicianship as much as they responded to my desire to worship God authentically. In other words, they wanted to go where I was going spiritually. Spiritual leadership is more important than musical leadership.

Karen Lafferty

Karen Lafferty is probably best known in the Christian world as the author of the Scripture chorus "Seek Ye First." This chorus has been key in opening doors to take her music around the world. Karen helped pioneer contemporary Christian music during the "Jesus Movement" in the 1970s as one of the first musicians with the California based record company Maranatha! Music.

As Karen's ministry led her outside of the U.S., she began to see the incredible potential of using contemporary Christian music to reach youth for Christ. In 1980 Karen founded Musicians For Missions International (MFMI) as part of Youth With A Mission (YWAM) in Amsterdam, Holland. The activities of MFMI have ranged from short-term mission trips to full-time staff "musicianaries" to a School of Music in Missions as part of YWAM's University of the Nations.

Karen returned to her U.S. home in 1996 and now directs MFMI from Santa Fe, New Mexico. Today, after three decades in Christian music, Karen continues to have much vision to train and mobilize musicians, lead worship, minister through concerts, write and record songs, and encourage others to "seek first the Kingdom of God."

Simple Praise Simply Draws
People to Jesus

It was April, 1979, when I found myself in Athens, Greece, with about 200 other young people from 15 different countries. Each one of us had been part of a Youth With A Mission (YWAM) Discipleship Training School (DTS) somewhere in Europe. My DTS was in Holland. Just a few days earlier I had arrived in Athens after a five day bus trip with the other DTS students for the outreach phase of our school.

Having already been in a full-time music ministry for eight years, I now felt the Lord was leading me to focus on using music in missions. During a three-month tour of Europe in 1978, I had seen firsthand that contemporary Christian music and worship were powerful tools to reach young people for Christ worldwide. It was amazing to me that even though I sang in English instead of their native European languages, that the youth would sit through a two hour concert and often respond to the Gospel message at the end. I became convinced that the primary reason for their interest was that I was doing a musical "style" they enjoyed. In reality, though, our strongest link was our human need to know and worship our Creator. As I shared about Christ through an interpreter and presented my songs, the Holy Spirit would speak to the hearts of the people. And now here I was in Athens asking God once again to use me to reveal Himself to the Greek people.

The Lord had already used the "internationalness" of my DTS to teach me many new things about music ministry and worship. The Europeans had encouraged me to play my oboe with the worship team. I had only played it with orchestras. What a joy to learn how to make my oboe an extension of my heart in worship of the Lord. I was also learning how sounds that had been so foreign to me like "Heer," which means "Lord" in Dutch, were taking on a heart meaning to me as I worshiped with the Dutch Christians.

It seemed like a normal outreach day as we headed out in mass to support the performance of "Toymaker and Son," a colorful pantomime which portrays the gospel. However, we soon realized that God wanted to touch the people of Athens in a different way that day. The Athens police decided we could not perform "Toymaker and Son" on the Athens University steps even though we had done it on several previous days. We were all very disappointed but asked God what we should do. This was the first time on the outreach that it was decided that we would split into smaller groups of about twenty and go to different parts of the city. I ended up with a group that simply stood in a quiet corner of a parking lot worshiping God in a very gentle manner. Even though our intention was simply to worship the Lord, not necessarily to draw a crowd, people began to come closer as they heard the songs of praise. As the people gathered I thought of Jesus' heart when he saw the multitudes and felt compassion because they were distressed and downcast like sheep without a shepherd (Mark 6:34). We decided not to preach that day, rather we told people that we would continue to sing songs of worship because God said that He would inhabit the praise of His people (Psalm 22:3) and that in His presence is the fullness of joy (Psalm 16:11). We explained that God wanted them to experience His love and joy that day. I can't even recall how long we continued to worship; but I remember another verse coming alive to me. Psalm 40:3 "And He put a new song in my mouth, a song of praise to our God; many will *see* and fear, and will trust in the Lord."

As some of us continued to worship, our leader invited any who had felt the presence of the Lord there and wanted to talk with one of us about Him to come forward. As many of them began to come forward to talk and pray with us, I once again saw how people long to be in God's presence. Worship can draw them into His presence, even on the busy streets of a crowded city. It wasn't just the "style" of music that drew them, but the Spirit that inhabited the music. We all witnessed firsthand how simple praise simply draws people to Jesus.

Rick Founds

Rick Founds has been leading worship since he was 14 years old. He has authored numerous songs that are used every week in church services worldwide. Some titles include "Lord, I Lift Your Name on High," "Jesus, Mighty God," "I Need You," and "Jesus, Draw Me Close."

Rick's educational and career activities are diverse, and include studies in music therapy, accounting, welding and machine sciences. He has a degree in radio media technology and experience in full-time ministry, over 12 years of full-time music ministry, research and development engineering in the fiber optics illumination industry, as well as a recent new church plant: "The Comfort Zone Ministries."

Rick lives in Southern California with his wife, three children, two cats and three fish (...used to be four fish, but...that's another story...).

Gruesome Worship

There was blood all over the guy's face. It was like something out of a Friday the 13th movie.

It was a hot, sweaty Thursday evening, smack in the middle of one of the warmest summers on record. The sanctuary was filled to capacity, and the air conditioning wasn't working all that well. This was one of those periodic special nights of worship. We would exchange the normal time allotted for in-depth study, with an extended time of praise, worship and prayer.

The Spirit of God was present in a very powerful way, despite the muggy conditions. Throughout the building, people were enthusiastically singing and worshiping the Lord. Most people had their eyes closed, some with hands raised, some standing in awe, some sitting, some quietly kneeling, as the worship team continued to lead with songs of gratitude and love to our Lord and Savior.

For the past few songs, I had been singing with my eyes closed, enjoying a particularly clear sense of the love and presence of Jesus. I became aware of a sound behind me, and slightly to my right. Turning my head in that direction, I opened my eyes. There was my drummer, head down, still quietly and sensitively keeping the beat, but his shoulders were trembling.

Wow. I thought. He is really in tune with the presence of God tonight. There he is, gently weeping as he worships God with skillful praise.

Then he looked up. He stared at me with pain in his eyes. The pain that only comes with trying to suppress extremely inappropriate laughter. He glanced toward the front row, just to my left. I followed his gaze.

The poor guy in the front row looked like he had just been pulled from a severe car accident! Blood in his hair. Blood smeared all over his forehead, cheeks and chin. Blood on what was once a nice blue shirt. Blood on one of the hands he had raised to the heavens.

Oh no! I thought to myself. We've got one of those wacko cult weirdos. One of these people like the ancient prophets of Baal, who thinks he needs to mutilate himself in order to be heard by God. Great. Now what? My drummer had nearly bitten off his own tongue to keep from laughing, but he kept on playing. Miraculously, nobody else seemed to have noticed yet. I thought to myself, "Better do another sing-to-the-Lord-with-your-eyes-closed type of song 'till I can get some help here."

Finally I began to understand what was happening. It was hot. It was sweaty. This guy had some kind of scab on his neck. Maybe from a cut or scrape. Maybe it was a giant zit. I don't know, but there it was. It had been itching, and he'd been scratching. It was a morbidly fascinating thing to watch. I observed with great wonder, as I continued to sing the melody and lyric of the current song. (An interesting experience, kind of like juggling with your brain.) There he sat, with eyes closed and hands lifted. From all indications, his heart was comfortably situated before the throne of God. What he was completely unaware of, was the fact that as he would unconsciously respond to the itch on his neck, he would uncoagulate his wound, collect a fresh supply of blood on his palm and fingers, rub his hand across his face, through his hair, and finally across the front of his shirt. Then reverently lift his hand once again in honor to the God of Heaven.

I was able to get the attention of one of the other singers on stage. I indicated with my head in the direction of the activity in the front row. She read my mind and quietly slipped off stage and quickly made her way to the nearby kitchen area. She returned in a flash with a moistened dish towel and managed to graciously make the gentleman aware of his situation. His face took on that priceless expression of perplexed shock, as he opened his eyes to the sight of his own bloody hand. Fortunately, he had the presence of mind not to scream. He thankfully accepted the damp towel, and quietly disappeared. Shortly thereafter he slipped back into the sanctuary. His face was scrubbed clean, he wore a lightweight windbreaker over his stained shirt, and a large bandage on his neck. Our friend resumed worship as if nothing had happened.

"Let's all stand and sing," I said, "Open our eyes Lord, we want to see Jesus."

Steve Phifer

Rev. Steve Phifer is a native of West Helena, Arkansas. Steve has a master's degree in music education from Wichita State University and has served as minister of music in Assemblies of God churches in Arkansas, Kansas and North Carolina. From 1993-95 he served the national music department of the Assemblies of God as the field representative for Worship and the Arts. In the fall of 1995 he joined the faculty of Southeastern College of the Assemblies of God in Lakeland, Florida, where he was chairman of the worship department of the college. In 1997 he took the position of worship and arts pastor at Suncoast Cathedral in St. Petersburg, Florida, marking his return to the pastoral music ministry.

Steve is president of Healing Streams Ministries, Inc., a nonprofit organization that encourages true worship through teaching and music. Under the banner of Worship Arts Resources he provides teaching materials, songs and orchestrations for worship and original dramatic scripts. He is the composer of several widely-used worship songs including, "In Your Presence," "A Healing Stream" and "Manifest Your Glory."

Steve and his wife, Freeda, have been married for 24 years and have two daughters, Nicole and Jennifer.

As a Daughter to Her Daddy— Minister to the Lord

Before I became a worship leader the phrase "minister to the Lord" intrigued me, but I didn't understand it. I first heard the phrase as part of the narration of a musical, "Come Together" by Jimmy and Carol Owens. Every time the words were used something stirred within me, but it was a contradictory sensation. On one hand it made no sense to me. However, on the other hand, I could not dismiss it. It was as if the Lord was telling me, "You don't understand this now, but someday you will." Little could I know then that this truth would become the main engine that powered all my ministry machines.

The problem was my concept of ministry. Growing up in a southern, small-town, classic-Pentecostal culture, I had developed the idea that ministry always involved the strong helping the weak. Ministry happened when a pastor, deacon, or at least a mature believer, would lay hands on someone with a problem to pray for them or counsel with them. From his or her position of power, the ministering party would impart strength, wisdom, faith or some other missing quality to the person in need. When would God ever be in need of ministry from me? How could He be weak and I strong? It didn't make any sense to me.

As a teenager I had been called to "the ministry." It was to be my life. Of course, I was certain that this meant that I was supposed to be strong for the weak, wise for the unwise, informed for the uninformed and so on. I had received the fullness of the Holy Spirit so He could flow through me like a river and bless the people who came in contact with me. I was to learn the Scriptures so I could always give an answer. I was to go to Bible college to sharpen this call, this mind, and this heart, so that I could be strong, even superior, so that I could minister to people.

The Lord preempted my Bible college plans and sent me instead to a small state college to major in music. With a call to preach, but an assignment to get a music education degree, it seemed natural for me to pour my concept of ministry into my musical preparation. I would become a versatile, superior musician, one who was so good, he could minister to people with music regardless of what kind of music they liked. I would do it all, every style on the map.

After a few years as a public school band director, I started my life as a minister of music. For the first five years (from 1975-1980) the only worship leading I did was altar music. Even today, prayer music is a favorite form of worship leading for me. But for those first five years that was almost all the worship leading I did. I served in classic Pentecostal churches that were not really into worship except around and about the altar. During that time, I learned much about how songs can flow together and about following the leadership of the Holy Spirit. However, I was ministering to those who were at the altar praying. My concept had not changed.

In 1980 I moved to a new state, a new region of the country, and into a new church that was heavily influenced by the charismatic renewal. For the first time in nine years of music teaching and ministry I was asked to regularly lead the worship time before the message. I had such a hunger in my heart for the presence of the Lord. I was convinced that this was the essence of my Pentecostal heritage and that we were in danger of losing it. I sensed that the visitation of God was not limited to history, not my personal history, not that of the local church, not even that of my denomination. God wanted to meet with us each time we gathered, and it all had something to do with worship, corporate worship. I knew there had to be more to it than singing a few fast songs and then a few slow songs. I was not satisfied with formulas that "worked." I wanted to understand. I asked the Lord to open my heart and mind to the subject of worship. He did.

One of the first things He opened to me was this concept of ministering to the Lord. A teacher, Roxanne Brant, came to our church. She was a tall, elegant lady who taught the Word of God. She was teaching a seminar on knowing God's will, but one of her books was *Ministering to the Lord—A Vision, A Search, A Discovery*. I was amazed! Someone had written a book on ministering to the Lord! I consumed her book. The truths in it changed my life. I discovered that the church had a three-fold purpose: to minister to the Lord through worship, to the church itself through fellowship and discipleship, and to the world through evangelism. I was thirty years old and had been a credentialed preacher since I was eighteen, but I had never been told about the three-fold mission of the church. I had never known that worship was the most important thing. Although I knew I was supposed to think that, I was secretly more comfortable ministering to the saints. I was a teacher and enjoyed watching my students grow in the Lord and in music. Ministry to the Lord was a foreign concept. But, if it was the first of three essential ministries of the church, I decided I had better learn what it meant to minister to the Lord. The fact is I can and I must minister to the Lord! But how could I minister to God? Did God have needs that I could meet? It was clear that my mind and my concept of ministry would have to expand to include ministry to God.

The mind-expander was named Nicole. Our oldest daughter came along in the late 70's and by 1980 she was one of those loving daughters who makes glad the heart of her dad. There it was! That is what ministry to the Lord is like! I was in every way superior to Nicole; I was bigger, stronger, smarter (when she became a teenager this was no longer true!), and wiser than a three-year-old girl. But did she minister to me? Yes! When she reached for me, when she asked for me, when she wanted to be with me, when she wanted to please me, that little girl, inferior though she may have been, ministered to the heart of her big, superior father. So much for the great ministering to the small!

In 1982 another little girl, Jennifer, came along. In a few years I could hear her running down the hall of the house with, "Daddy's home!" at the top of her voice, while I was still in the front porch! The fact and example is this: loving children minister to loving parents like no one else can. A person in music and worship ministry is apt to hear a lot of compliments from people, but the acclaim and appreciation of our children is the most meaningful.

Once, a few years later, I was off somewhere to teach about worship. I found a note that Jennifer left for me. To fully understand this you must understand how she felt about her room. It was her domain and her hiding place. She had organized all her stuffed animals in perfect order and they served her faithfully. Her note to me ended something like this, "And I love you, Daddy, more than anything in my room." She ministered to me. She exalted me to the pinnacle of her world, above all its other inhabitants.

Worshipers are children of the Heavenly Father. Jesus spoke of God as Father more than any other way. Here is the illustration of our interaction with God. Not only does He deal with us and provide for us as a perfect Father, He responds to us as a perfect Father also. "If we being earthy fathers know how to give..." the Scripture says. It does no damage to Scripture to extend that to "If we being earthly fathers know how to receive love from our children, how much more does our Heavenly Father receive the love of His children." Why else would Jesus exalt loving the Father to the highest privilege of human kind and the highest duty of man? It is to this ministry that we are to bring "heart, soul, mind, and strength." This is the object of the first four commandments. This is the great conclusion to which the wise King Solomon came after spending his life in experimentation with alternative sources of happiness.

My life's job description became Psalm 29:1,2: "Give unto the Lord, O ye Mighty. Give unto the Lord glory and strength. Give unto the Lord the glory due unto His name. Worship the Lord in the beauty of holiness." I made this the foundation stone of all my ministry. Every song, every service, every project, every production, every rehearsal, would be measured by "the glory due unto His name." I gathered to my side, singers and players, artists of all kinds, who had their hearts set on pleasing God, on ministering to Him. Mary of Bethany became our role model. She and Martha made the Lord feel welcome in their house, ministering to Him. She lavished her best gift on Him. She did what she could. The Lord Jesus received her personally-given ministry with these words, "She has done a beautiful thing to Me" (Matthew 26:10).

That became the goal of every artist in our fellowship: personal ministry to the Lord. Bringing pleasure to the heart of the Father through our ministry was what brought us the most pleasure.

The Scriptures told me about ministering to the Lord. My children taught me how. Throughout the years I have seen the benefits. It is no wonder loving God is the first and greatest commandment. As I have said countless times just before leading worship, "Let us focus all our love and attention on the Lord. Let us give unto Him the glory due His Name!"

Doug Hanks

Doug Hanks consults with mainline Protestant churches making the transition to contemporary worship from more traditional forms—a task that is always demanding and never boring. Doug holds a master's degree in theology from Fuller Theological Seminary in Pasadena, California, and a bachelor's in communication arts (television production) from California Polytechnic Institute (Cal Poly), Pomona, California.

Doug reviews worship music for Worship Leader *magazine and has also contributed articles to that publication. Published music with Maranatha! Music, his original praise songs like "I Am the Resurrection" and "Spirit of Power" are sung around the world.*

For fun, Doug writes country music (he's an active member of the Nashville Songwriters Association International), and he also enjoys film studies and cultivates bonsai trees.

Doug lives in Claremont, California, with his wife, Claire, and three cats—Buckminster, Nigel and Matt.

Worshiping God at the Oasis

———⟨◎⧘⧘⧘⧘⊙⟩———

Worship is responding to God, but God never promised that worship would happen only on Sunday during neatly planned, well-organized services within the comfortable confines of a church building. God leads His own worship service whenever and wherever He wants to lead it—even if the opportunity to worship takes place on a week day in the middle of the Arizona desert near midnight at a modern oasis—the interstate rest stop.

On the Wednesday evening before Thanksgiving, my wife, Claire, my brother, Phil, and I loaded our car and headed out Interstate 10 from southern California toward Arizona to spend the weekend with my mom in Sun City, a retirement community west of Phoenix. The trip generally takes a little more than six hours. We left at sundown, planning to pull in at mom's house around midnight. The halogen star fields of suburban California neighborhoods faded into the crisp, dark desert night where we could see the stars as God made them. We passed the time catching up on each others' lives and talking about the food we would eat, the golf we would play, and the danger we would experience driving the golf cart and dodging large American-made cars on the streets of the planned community.

We crossed the Colorado River which separates California and Arizona, and passed successfully through the fruit inspection station ("Do you have any fruits or nuts?" "Only my brother in the back seat!"). From there, the freeway makes a slow climb through some hills and levels off into the rocky Arizona landscape which is broken only by the characteristic saguaro cacti, the kind you see in John Wayne movies. About an hour east of the border, sits a rest stop—a necessary one. We pulled into the parking lot about ten o'clock and joined a dozen weary travelers and a few long haul truckers.

As I stepped out of the car, I saw a pickup truck pull into the rest stop and park a few spaces away. Thinking it was just another traveler seeking relief, I stood and stretched out the cramps from driving. The last thing I expected at that rest stop was to meet anyone I knew, but over my shoulder I heard a young woman's voice, "You go to New Hope, don't you?!"

At the time, I was worship leader at New Hope Community Church, a contemporary, seeker-sensitive church in Rancho Cucamonga, California, a commuter suburb located about forty miles east of Los Angeles. The church vibrated every weekend with exciting spiritual growth that paralleled the rapid growth experienced by the sleepy desert city. One of the people attending worship every week was Ted, a recovering addict whose spiritual journey had led him straight into the arms of Jesus. Ted wore his long hair in a pony tail and his chest-length beard hid most of his face which was lined with the hardness of life. But Ted's clear, blue eyes reflected the changes present in his soul. On a rare occasion, Ted's daughter accompanied him to worship services.

Vashti, a seeker, came with her dad and was in church on that particular Sunday before Thanksgiving. I don't remember seeing her there (which makes me think I must have been asleep). She was a child of the nineties. Her multi-colored hair framed a fresh, attractive face that was pierced in two places. The theme of the service that week pertained to being thankful to God for the things He does for us. As part of that service I led "Give Thanks." One of the lines we sang together was "Let the weak say I am strong because of what the Lord has done." I don't know if Vashti sang those words, but she heard them. She was about to be very thankful for His provision, and I was about to learn an important truth about God's sovereignty and timing.

Stop and consider the odds: I just got out of my car and I'm standing at a particular rest stop in the middle of nowhere in Arizona on a specific day at a specific time of that day. The odds of such a thing happening still astound me today. A hundred things could have altered that situation. My brother could have been caught in traffic and not arrived at the time he did at our house to prepare to leave. We could have taken a few more minutes to pack. We could have lingered at the Golden Arches in Blythe instead of just getting Diet Cokes. I could have driven three miles per hour faster or three miles per hour slower and arrived twelve minutes earlier or twelve minutes later. Any one of those factors could have altered the time that I arrived at the rest stop. But it didn't. I arrived when God wanted me to arrive. Even more astonishing is the fact that God used me to answer Vashti's prayer.

Vashti was on her way to spend the weekend with her fiancé in Phoenix. Her compact truck had been running on fumes for thirty minutes and she had been praying that she wouldn't run out of gas and be stranded on the shoulder of the road. Such a thing is dangerous, but especially harrowing on a lonely interstate in the middle of the desert for a woman traveling alone. She pulled into the rest stop hoping to find someone who was carrying some extra gasoline with them so she could continue her journey. Needless to say, she was relieved to see a familiar face—the face of a pastor. She knew God was answering her prayer.

Now it was my turn to worship and obediently respond to God's person and work. He had provided a free way to His Son years before with an endless supply of fuel—His Spirit. The solution was a simple one: We learned from some people at the rest stop that there was a gas station just seven miles ahead. Vashti headed down the road with the needle still pointing to "E" on her gauge, but with new confidence that right behind her was a car to pick her up if she became stranded. She made it to the gas station, she filled up her truck, and I paid for it just to remind her that God meets all our needs in times of trouble. She thanked me profusely and she disappeared into the night.

I haven't seen Vashti since that night, but every time I see her dad he shares that she speaks often about her ordeal and the night that God answered her prayer in the middle of an interstate in Arizona. Every time I stop at that rest stop, I remember that the people worshiping God every week are the people He wants to be there and that God leads His own worship service whenever and wherever He wants to—even at a modern oasis in the desert.

Gary Shelton

While still in his teens, Gary Shelton's giftings pointed him to a musical career in the secular realm. After years of turmoil, his life turned when he was led into a saving relationship with Jesus Christ by Anni. Shortly thereafter they married and the Savior's supernatural plan for Gary began to unfold.

In 1993, the Lord spoke to the Sheltons' hearts, calling them to full-time ministry and miraculously answering their financial needs when they left their secular jobs. After founding Skywork, a nonprofit organization dedicated to supporting the Sheltons' itinerant music ministry, Gary traveled extensively, leading worship in services from Toronto to London.

Since the birth of Skywork, Gary has produced four popular worship recordings: "In the Presence of the Lord," "Times of Refreshing," "Catch the Fire" and "Torn Together." The ever-expanding acceptance of his contemporary style and traditional themes is testimony to the Lord's movements in Gary's musical ministry.

Gary is currently one of the worship leaders at the St. Louis Vineyard, where he attends with his wife and four children.

Little "David" to the Rescue

Thinking back over the past ten years, I have had many occasions to experience the Lord as Jehovah-Jireh. When on the road leading worship for renewal meetings, I've been given many opportunities to cry out for God's help and His supernatural provision. He has always been faithful!

As I relate this particular story, it's important for you to understand that as far as gifts go, administration is at the bottom of my list. The reason you need to know this is because the Lord has covered for my lack of organizational abilities innumerable times by providing players, equipment, and helpers. There was one time however, when I really felt well prepared. I had a full team of skilled players. We had managed to squeeze in a decent practice the night before. The sound check went smoothly. I even had people to run the overhead projectors. Everything seemed to be taken care of. Then came the twist.

Sixty minutes before we were to begin leading a meeting of about 1000 people, the drummer was hit hard with a severe case of stage fright. The idea of playing in front of that many people was apparently very intimidating, so he told me he wasn't going to be able to play. I was really bummed but I realized there was only one thing to do: break into some major intercession. My prayers were very deep and profound. If I recall correctly, I prayed something along the lines of, "Oh my God, *help*!!!"

The great part was that God had already visited my future and though I was totally unprepared, He was—as always—totally prepared to deal with this impending crisis. I asked the rest of the team if any of them could play drums for the night. No one else on the team played drums. However, the guy who was the church's regular worship leader said he had a son who played. I asked him if he would be willing to go get his son so that I could talk to him. I was extremely confused when the guy showed up with this sweet looking kid who I figured to be about 11 years old, 12 at the most. I had been expecting him to appear with his grown son. However, I quickly remembered 1 Samuel 16:7, "The LORD does not look at the things man looks at. Man looks at the outward appearance, but the LORD looks at the heart." God knew that this kid had everything it took to release faith and exuberance in the people there that night.

I asked the boy, "Do you think you can play these drums?

"Yes," he responded.

I replied, "Then you're my man!" and we proceeded with our preparations for leading worship.

This young man had not been at the practice we held the night before, nor had he heard many of the songs that were on the song list for the evening. He was so young that he practically had to stand up to hit the cymbals. However, the Lord resided mightily in that young man!!! Worship was powerful that night, and both God and I knew that it had very little to do with me.

The Lord sent this young "David" into the battle to help fight off my "Goliath" of the night. The kid was a total blessing—to God, to the congregation and perhaps mostly to me. Who would have thought that God would answer my prayers with an 11-year-old? As always, though, the Lord did abundantly more than I could think, ask, hope or pray for!

Geoff Thurman

Geoff Thurman began crafting songs in 1976. He found commercial success in 1984. His first published release was recorded by Amy Grant, "Jehovah," which topped the charts in October of that year and stayed there for three months. He has nearly 1,000 songs published. Of his 200 recorded songs (20 songs in the top ten), many have been performed by Grammy and Dove-nominated artists like Glen Campbell, Ricky Skaggs, Four Him, First Call, Pam Thum, Michael English, Bruce Carroll, Cindy Morgan, Sierra, Point of Grace, and Phillips, Craig & Dean. He has produced records for Glen Campbell and recorded with Ricky Skaggs on such ground-breaking projects as "Silent Witness." He is presently published by the Gaylord Entertainment Group.

Geoff is working with Bob Kilpatrick (author of "Lord Be Glorified") on a new vehicle to take the Gospel to the streets—a project called "Songs for God" (worship for the unsaved). He is also currently working on a Broadway musical called "Real Life" with stars from "Sunset Boulevard."

Geoff, his wife, Becky, and their daughter, Naomi, live in Murfreesboro, Tennessee.

The Journey of Worship

As I think back to remember what was special about leading worship in the days when we didn't know what worship leading was, I am reminded of what my wife and I were taught by the musicians of that day. We learned that there was a need to look at worship as a progression. It is first necessary to inform one's self that God is about to be worshiped. However, there is a process that begins and continues in worship. I view it from the passage of Scripture that says, "Come and let us go up to the mountain of the LORD..." (Micah 4:2).

I take great care in planning a trip. I find it essential to know how far it is and how long it will take me to travel there. I also must know what to do or say once I arrive at my destination. At some point in the journey up the hill to the mountain of the Lord, I am faced with the reality that I am not truly prepared to meet and be with my God. I realize that, like the prophet Isaiah, I am a man of unclean lips and I must be cleansed to honestly enter His presence and meet with Him. Confession is my way to prepare to meet the Lord face to face. I have found that I cannot truly worship without recognizing that I must first be made clean to stand before God. The interesting twist is that it is only by God that I am made clean. I cannot do it on my own. It is only His grace that makes me clean.

I have also come to realize that the trip must be accepted by the church. A close friend of mine, a song-writing partner and a worship leader in middle Tennessee, was instrumental in helping me learn this lesson. My family and I were attending a small church near our home. We had not been at this church for very long and had no desires to be a part of worship teams (or any other leadership type position, for that matter).

At one point I invited the pastor and his family to come to a live recording of a worship service that I was involved with producing. After the service he realized that I had a vision for worship that he felt was needed by his church. The pastor went back to the board of directors and asked to have me installed as music minister for this church. I struggled with the idea of a position I didn't want to accept and felt tied to a runaway locomotive headed into the train station loaded with fireworks (some fun, eh?).

My friend counseled me to stay at the church, accept the position for a time, and see if God was planting me there. The test was not to see if the people would respond to changing styles of worship (from gentle Maranatha-type choruses to full-out rock and roll with horns and choirs). The test was to see if God ordained this vision for this body. If they were unwilling to go up the mountain with me then perhaps we missed something along the way.

If I change the vision of worship God has given me to please people, then I am in error and must repent. If I lead the worship according to what God has shown me His vision for worship is and they respond favorably, then the body is on a path toward change (although that change can sometimes take a lifetime to achieve).

We must go up the mountain together, exalting Him with our worship.

Steve Cook

Steve Cook oversees the music publishing for PDI Ministries, a church planting and oversight organization. Steve is an accomplished keyboardist, arranger and songwriter. He and his wife, Vikki, have written numerous popular songs such as "Great Are You, Lord," "Raise Up an Army" and "We Rejoice in the Grace of God." Steve has also been instrumental in the entire recording/production of more than 20 recordings for PDI. Additionally, he and Vikki serve on the worship team of Covenant Life Church in Gaithersburg, Maryland.

An avid reader, Steve's favorite authors include John Piper, Jonathan Edwards and Charles Spurgeon. He also enjoys playing softball and collecting baseball cards.

Steve and Vikki have been married for 18 wonderful years and have two beautiful daughters, Stephanie and Suzanna. They live in Gaithersburg.

"You gave us... death?!?"

Not long ago I had an experience in one of my church's home group meetings which was a humorous reminder of the importance of theology in worship. Content *does* matter.

We were at a friend's home, standing in a circle, being led in an intimate time of worship. Our worship leader that evening possessed a strong voice, which can be a very valuable asset in these non-amplified settings. As it turned out, his strong voice was also a key factor in the way events unfolded in the moments ahead.

Several songs into our time of worship we were singing a song entitled "Holy Love." The focus of this song is on God's love for us displayed on the cross. The opening lyrics of the chorus are "What holy love, enduring death, You gave us life. What holy love, Lord, we're amazed with You..." On this particular evening as we all sang with eyes closed and hands raised, our worship leader's passionate voice could be heard above all of our's exclaiming "What holy love, enduring life, You gave us death..." The lyric change was jolting and I immediately opened my eyes. Others obviously had the same reaction and several were looking around with a look of smirkish shock. This, as you may well imagine, gave way to thunderous laughter at our worship leader's mistake. He eventually realized what he had said, and, unfortunately, our intimate worship came to an abrupt, though memorable ending.

Such a mistake is not uncommon. We've all made them. However, these events can serve to remind us that the content of our worship does matter. Jesus instructed us to worship "in spirit and in truth." This "truth" is the character and deeds of God. Truth is what fuels the fire of passionate worship. As we incorporate songs that are rich in content—songs about the cross, the sovereignty of God or the grace of God, for example—we are spreading before the people we lead a feast of truth that feeds the hungry heart and fills it with glorious affections for God. This truth is a means of God revealing Himself and a means of His changing us to be more conformed to His image.

It's true that different songs serve different roles in worship and not all of our songs will be bursting with deep theological content. However, we would serve our people well to be sure that we provide for them, frequently during worship, rich portions of truth that fill their minds and hearts with some aspect of the character and works of our wondrous God. It is at this table of truth that God will be glorified and we will be satisfied with Him.

Bruce Harry Larson

Bruce Harry Larson has been involved in worship ministries for 23 years, with 16 of those years at First Assembly of God in Fargo, North Dakota, where he serves as minister of music. Bruce has also served in associate positions in Billings, Montana, and Fort Worth, Texas.

Bruce has led worship seminars throughout the region and has written many praise and worship choruses such as "Lord, I'm Hungry," "I've Come to Praise Him" and "We are the Army." Bruce also writes and directs several musical drama productions that are seen by thousands every year. While he lived in Fort Worth, Bruce led worship for James Robison's conferences around the country.

Bruce enjoys bicycling and is an avid roller coaster fanatic. Married for 22 years, Bruce and his wife, Marsha, have three children, Heidi, Quinn and Bryce.

"Yah! Sure... ya' betcha"

"As I walked through the wilderness, I alighted in a certain place..." So begins John Bunyan in his classic, "The Pilgrim's Progress." He then takes us on a journey past such aptly named places as Christian Falls, the Valley of Humiliation, Delectable Mountains, and the Enchanted Grounds. In each place, the pilgrim learns subtle, yet life changing lessons. I, too, am on a journey, but somehow I got stuck in the land of "Yah! Sure...ya' betcha."

This fantastic journey actually began many, many years ago. Well, twenty years to be exact. I was graduating from a Bible college in Minneapolis and had already accepted the position of youth and music pastor in a far-off city just south of the North Pole called Fargo. (Okay, it's actually south of the Canadian Border, but not by much!) Our commencement speaker was delivering an excellent challenge to the graduating class and used one of the most classic examples of submitting to the call of God. He began by saying that some of us would not really suffer that much for the Kingdom. Some of us would go to Hawaii, the Caribbean, or the Bahamas. After this he went on to say that indeed some of us would suffer greatly, having to endure hardships and tremendous inconveniences, because some would be called to such places as the African

Sahara Desert, the Russia Siberia, or even Fargo, North Dakota!

As my classmates turned and gazed at me, I didn't know whether to puff my chest out or fall on my knees and cry out, "Why me, God? I think I can handle Hawaii. But Fargo??!"

As with many obscure, out-of-the-way places, Fargo is usually only referred to in three instances:

1.) The whole city is wiped out by a natural disaster.

2.) A darkly murderous movie is made with a title of the same name, but which actually has little or nothing to do with Fargo itself.

3.) You happen to have a second cousin to your uncle's brother's sister-in-law who is Norwegian and lives in Fargo.

And what, you may ask, does this have to do with worship? Everything if you look at worship leading as a call of God.

Unfortunately, in many ways we have measured success like the world. The bigger the church and city we are in, the more we appear successful. Our goal seems to have become encased in the plastic unreality of becoming a recognized national name. If we could just release the right worship CD or be the featured worship leader at some prestigious conference, then we could consider ourselves successful. Yet, all we have done is enter what one very thoughtful author termed the "Great American Worship Competition."

Please understand me, I am very grateful for the different voices God has raised up to speak on a national platform. However, we must see that God must raise us up and not our own need for success-oriented gratification. When we seek for human recognition, our worship leading will be based only on what the current style and trend happens to be and not on what God has ordained for our community and our congregation. We can begin to become manipulative and self-absorbed in producing feelings more than faith. We can begin to determine the success of a service on how good the band sounded, how "hot" the singers were, or how loud the congregation yelled.

Let me explain that I like those things as much as the next person, but they should not be the "goal" of worship. The goal is to bring people into the very presence of God, however that is manifested. My goal in sharing this is to relate a necessary ingredient in the spiritual success of any worship leader: faithfulness.

Faithfulness is even more important than talent. We live in an age where talent is almost worshiped and some have put a premium on talent above faithfulness. Unfortunately, talent will not go to the hospital to minister to a music team member. Faithfulness will. Talent will not pray for the senior pastor. Faithfulness will. Talent survives only on the platform, faithfulness can be seen in the most humble places. Talent does not always need the anointing to stir emotions, but talent with faithfulness not only stirs emotions, but can be used to soften bitter hearts, bring release from depression, even provide a healing environment in the presence of God.

Faithfulness brings an understanding of reliability, integrity, and trust. But I also believe that faithfulness brings with it an understanding of longevity. Some of the most profound lessons I have learned have come as a result of being in one place (Fargo) for sixteen years. Yes, they were painful and sometimes overwhelming lessons, but the view from the other side is awesome.

Here are some of the advantages to having stayed in one place for a long period of time:

✓ I have a vision for our community which coincides with the pastor's vision. It used to be that the average stay for assistant pastors was one and one half to two years. It takes almost three years for you to truly know and understand the people in your church, let alone in the community. My senior pastor has been at this church for 27 years and still has a fresh vision to touch this area with the gospel of Jesus Christ. My longevity has allowed me the blessing of developing the music and worship ministries to flow in that vision in a way that would not have happened otherwise.

✓ I have earned the trust of our board of deacons. Not just because of what I have done right, but also because they have been able to see how I've handled my mistakes. There is a more trusting environment that increases the board's willingness to invest finances because of a long track record.

✓ I am able to minister to our congregation on a level of reality. Longevity has a tendency to destroy all pedestals people may try to put us on. They see how I've changed or handled family situations. They trust me to walk with them through difficulties because they've seen me struggle and yet still lift up praises.

✓ I am able to minister to our community from a level of trust. People outside the church walls are generally skeptical of what happens inside the church walls. Longevity has allowed for unique opportunities. Because of our dramatic productions we have performed over the years, I have had opportunities to speak to drama classes, serve as an advisor for a community youth arts council, and even host our community symphony and opera company in our building. I even performed in one of our university's ballet productions (believe me, you don't want the details). But even more importantly, I have been able to pray with neighbors and touch other ministries in this community because they know I'm committed and called to this area.

✓ I have to continually be creative. Longevity will force you to run out of ideas. No...seriously...that's good! We could continually move from situation to situation simply relying on what we have always done. That will work only for a short time and robs us of the times of calling out to God for help and seeing the awesome results. I can no longer approach each service with the idea that this is going to work because it always has. Longevity brutally took me past that point and that has allowed God to re-lease creativity in me as I have cried out to Him. I have had to rely more on times of spiritual renewal than times of pull-ing out an "oldie." I have learned that God's faithfulness will always go farther than my own faithfulness.

Some have asked if it is possible to stay too long. I have asked myself that countless times over these years. I have found that when I do, I go to the Lord and He is always faithful to order my steps. The process of self-analysis is sometimes unnecessary and can produce deep self-inflicted wounds. I have learned to trust my Lord. I will always have weaknesses. I will most likely continue to make mistakes. But one thing I know is that God will be faithful to the call-ings and giftings He has placed in my life. I can learn from these times and continue to change because I do not feel the need to run from them. God will close doors and open doors and grant me the wisdom and cunning to follow the Holy Spirit.

Fargo is my place of calling right now. I am so at peace here. Do I enjoy two hundred feet of snow and ninety below zero temperatures? Are you nuts? Do I enjoy eagle-sized mosquitoes and two-week long summers? Okay, maybe I'm exaggerating. The mosquitoes are only the size of robins. But I love the people. I love this area. I love the call of God. I love Fargo. Yah! Sure...ya' betcha!

Shawn Craig

Shawn Craig has served in music ministry for over 18 years. A prolific song writer, he is probably best known for his song, "In Christ Alone," which won the Dove Award for Song of the Year in 1993. As a member of the contemporary singing group, Phillips, Craig & Dean, he has traveled extensively throughout the United States, ministering in churches of various backgrounds.

He is also author of a new devotional book, "Between Sundays," published by Howard Publishing.

Shawn currently serves as worship leader and music pastor for South County Christian Center in St. Louis, Missouri.

God Is not Surprised!

When I read chapters 3 and 4 of the book of Exodus, I can't help but smile a little at Moses and his doubtfulness. God chose Moses to be the leader of a nation, yet Moses seems to be more than a little surprised at what God is calling him to do. "But suppose they will not believe me or listen to my voice…" (Exodus 4:1).

The reason I smile when I read this is that I see myself in the calling of Moses. In fact, I never cease to be surprised at the way God has continued to expand my vision along the way.

As a teen, I knew that God had called me to some sort of full-time service. But the only evidence of gifting was my love for music. I would practice singing and playing for hours, with dreams of being an accomplished musician. My time with the Lord was often filled with a hunger for His presence, but I had no definite sense of how my love for music would fit into God's plans for my life.

I recall one older saint saying to me, "Keep up the consecration, son. One day you will preach the Word." I remember thinking, "What a confused lady. I know my gifts and I know my limitations. She recognizes God's calling on my life but obviously doesn't know I am called to be a musician."

As a young man in Bible school in central California, I studied music and began to realize that not only could I continue in music but it could be a ministry as well. I took a part-time job in a local church and was thrilled to be involved in music every day even though it was a struggle financially. I remember a lot of pbj sandwiches. My greatest struggle, though, came with the leadership aspect of being a music director. Because of my own lack of self-confidence, I found it most difficult to bear the responsibility. I felt unequipped and unworthy of the call. Yet, God seemed to add to instead of take away the challenges.

It was a couple of years after my tenure there that I discovered the renewal that was taking place in praise and worship. It was like a wonderful breath of fresh air. I loved the new choruses and the passion with which people sang. The songs I heard were much different from those to which I had become accustomed, but I loved the lyrics. They were so intimate toward God. They were less body-directed and more Christ-centered. I knew there was much more for me to learn, and I sensed God calling me onward.

The journey from musician to music director to music pastor/worship leader was a difficult one for me. Each time that I sensed the Spirit moving me out of my comfort zone, I would resist. Each new challenge would take me by surprise and I would be aware of my own inadequacies. But with the help of supportive pastors and friends, I would cautiously walk through each new door.

God would meet me each time, giving me the ability to take each leap of faith.

Soon I found myself entering a new reality in worship. I began to experience a wonderful flow of the Spirit in my personal devotion time as I worshiped at His feet. It wasn't long before I had an overwhelming desire to help others experience the power of true worship, pointing them to a Christ who not only wanted to save them but to enjoy them, to love them intimately.

Now I find myself not only leading praise and worship but also teaching and preaching—something that dear older saint had told me I would do years ago, though I could not envision it at the time.

It was after one mid-week Bible study that I recall a dear one who asked for prayer. With tearful emotion she said, "I don't know what to do. My children are grown and have their lives. I knew my purpose when they were at home. I worked hard to raise them in the knowledge of the Lord. Now, I don't know why I'm here. What is my purpose now? I can't believe I'm at this point in my life."

I remember feeling compassion for what she was going through and in a few moments hearing that small voice inside saying, "Tell her that I am not surprised." As I realized the depth of the meaning in those few words, I found great comfort for her and for myself. Although at times we are surprised at the circumstances of life or the call of the ministry, God is not. He is always ahead of us, preparing the way, ordering our steps and is never taken off guard. Never will we hear Him say, "What will I do now?" Instead, He lovingly looks at us and says, "Walk on, child. I know you're surprised, but I saw it coming and you are going to be just fine!"

God continues to stretch me. Now I say with joy, "Stretch on, Lord." He will continue to stretch you if you allow Him to. When your ministry is in His hands anything is possible. If you are walking in covenant with God, He will be faithful to meet you at a point just beyond your own self-imposed limits. He knows where you are. He knows the path you take. He is not anxious or weary. "The steps of a good man are ordered by the Lord" (Psalm 37:23).

"Oh, Father, Your ways are higher. It is good to know that although I may be surprised once in a while at my circumstances, You are never shocked or startled at life. You know the path I take and I cannot escape from Your presence. I know You have good plans for me."

Twila Paris

Twila Paris comes from an amazing Christian heritage. Her great-grandparents were ministers of the gospel and moved across the Southern Plains in the early part of the twentieth century setting up tent meetings and brush-arbor churches. Her grandparents were also pastors who started churches where none existed. As one church was planted and brought to the place of relative independence, they moved on to another place to repeat the process of building the church. Twila's dad is an ordained minister and for much of his ministry has worked with Youth With A Mission, working with people who carry the gospel all over the world.

Because Twila was brought up in a family employed in an itinerant ministry (she didn't live in a home with her own bedroom until she was seven), she was a "team" member as far back as she can remember. Her "team" job was to sing. Twila was the oldest of four children, and she began to "solo" sing in the team ministry by the time she was three. She cut her first record called "Twila Paris, America's Little Sweetheart" at eight.

Twila's worship songs like "He is Exalted," "We Bow Down" and "Lamb of God" have had a major impact on churches worldwide.

Every Heart that Is Breaking
Adapted from the book, *In This Sanctuary*
(published by Star Song, 1993)

My husband, Jack, has a good friend from college who got married shortly after we did. They keep up with each other as friends by going to dinner together every once in a while.

One night Jack's friend called and asked Jack to go to lunch with him the next day. Jack thought he sounded down in his spirits, but didn't press him about it on the phone, figuring if there was something wrong he would hear of it the next day.

Unfortunately, the news was not good. Before a year had gone by in the marriage, his bride decided she did not love him and had simply packed up and left him without notice or reason.

Being a newlywed myself, I was sickened by the tragic circumstances of Jack's friend. That night my sleep was restless and full of pain, so I got up, went alone into my music room, and in the early hours of the morning, I continued to think about the pain he was going through.

As I sat there meditating on his pain, I began to see the heart of God as it was turned toward Jack's friend and all the hurting people of the world. I know that God is fully aware of all the suffering people go through and that God can bring comfort and healing to their lives.

I began to think of different examples of hurting people, and the song "Every Heart That Is Breaking" came to me. For every line in that song I have a personal example: the mother and young boy who had recently lost a father, the fallen teenager and her devastated father, the son dying with AIDS, the hungry child, and the refugee. For them the message is that God sees you, and knows you, and loves you.

Worship ministers to the hurting people of the world because God is present in worship to bring a healing touch into our lives. A lot of people say, "Don't go to worship to get, go to worship to give." I think that is a half-truth.

We do go to worship to give glory and honor to God. But worship is a two-way action. God is there doing what God has done for us in Jesus Christ. In Christ, God conquered all the powers of evil and will ultimately, through the death and resurrection of Christ, bring healing to all the nations and all the world. Right now, in worship, God gives us a taste of His healing, a down payment on our eternal treasure.

So I think the church needs to be more sensitive to the hurting persons of the local congregation. I think the church needs to provide space within its worship for healing. It could be in songs, prayers, preaching, communion, or in a special act of anointing for healing. However a local church chooses to reach out to hurting people, a move in that direction is imperative.

Bill
Rayborn

William H. (Bill) Rayborn is president of TCMR Communications, Inc., and is editor and publisher of The Church Music Report, *a newsletter for church musicians.*

Bill is a native of Tulsa, Oklahoma, and a graduate of Oklahoma Baptist University with a bachelor's degree in music education. He has served as minister of music at churches in Oklahoma, Missouri, South Carolina, Texas and California. He was director of record promotion for Word, Inc., executive director for Andraé Crouch and the Disciples, vice president of Christian Artists Corporation, director of music publications for Tempo Music and general manager of MSI Press.

Bill's hobbies include photography, computers and music. He is married to the former Lynann Kurr, has four daughters and resides in Grapevine, Texas, a suburb of Dallas and Fort Worth.

Be Careful How You Button Your Coat

⊃═╫╫╫═⊂

While serving as minister of music at a church in South Carolina I came to realize that as church music and worship leaders, no matter where we are, people are watching us and following our example.

It was a Sunday morning when one of our children's choirs was scheduled to sing. The mother of an eight-year-old choir member came to me before the service with a strange request. "Mr. Rayborn, I hope you never do anything wrong."

I told her how much I shared her wish but asked why she would make such a statement. She then related this story:

It seems that they wanted their son to look his best for the choir program and had purchased a new suit for him to wear for the performance. As they got out of the car that morning, the mother asked the boy to button his coat. "Not right now, Mom" he replied. "I want to wait and see how Mr. Rayborn has his coat buttoned."

The Bible admonishes us to be an example for the believers. Those of us in leadership positions in the church need to understand we are being watched at all times. We need to be careful how we button our coats.

Beulah Land

———⟡———

One of my most favorite stories was told by Dr. Travis Shelton, professor at Southern Methodist University. He tells how, while directing the music at his church, he frequently had a request service as part of their congregational singing. One lady in his congregation was always first with a request—and it was always the same request: "Beulah Land" (Actually "Dwelling in Beulah Land").

Shelton says that one Sunday evening his choir was sitting at the front of the sanctuary when the lady made her regular request. He saw this as his chance to "teach her a lesson." In his very best dance-band style, he raced through the gospel song. The choir swayed from side to side, even raising their hands in mock pentecostal fashion on the little after-beat section of "Praise God." When he finished, the choir laughed. He was sure he had taught her a lesson and "Beulah Land" would be a problem no more.

Two days later, Dr. Shelton received two unsigned postcards, one of which he said "hangs over my desk to this day." It said plainly: "Dear Dr. Shelton, 'Beulah Land' is here to stay. You, ain't necessarily!"

There is a lesson to be learned here that goes far beyond "Dwelling in Beulah Land." We need to remember that we are servants of our congregations. While it could be argued that we should seek to expand the musical tastes (both up and down) of our people, we must never feel it is our place to raise the musical level of our congregation. We need to meet our people's needs where they are!

This is probably one of the best arguments for the so called "blended service" or "blended worship." We need to give our people variety so we can reach all of the people some of the time, not some of the people all of the time. Now, if you agree with this, let me add a word of caution. I've seen many allow the pendulum to swing too far one way. Just because praise and worship choruses appeal to many is no reason for a steady diet, thus neglecting some of the rich hymns, gospel songs and anthems of the past.

So, this is a plea for you to get to know your people and their needs—to do music that speaks to your people, not just to yourself. Don't allow your personal preferences to dictate your total direction. Otherwise, you may find someone saying they are here to stay... and you "ain't" necessarily!

A Tale of Two Churches

I recently received two church newsletters. Both were about the same size and appearance. Church #1 (a church of about 2,000 members in North Texas) carried a pastor's column where, at the end of a lengthy epistle, the pastor offered congratulations to a pastoral staff member (not the minister of music) on his anniversary with the church utilizing just two sentences.

Church #2, a church just slightly larger in Southern Florida also carried a lengthy pastor's column that took over 2/3 of an 8-1/2 x 11 page. Here the pastor raves about his minister of music in the entire column titled "Not Duration, But Donation." He says it's great to hang around for a long time. "Doing time is one thing, but it's the contribution of your life..."

The minister of music at church #2 just celebrated his 20th anniversary. The pastor wishes him the best for their future years together. The minister of music at church #1 was fired last week...the fourth such firing of a pastoral member in the past few years.

The moral I would suggest is that when you are in the process of choosing a position that you carefully consider not only the church, not only the salary, but also the history of the church and history of the senior pastor. Talk with former staff members both of the church and of the pastor's former churches *before* you accept the position.

While we need to be sensitive to God's calling from one church to another, He has given us intelligence to be able to learn from the past. It's been said that those who refuse to learn from history are destined to repeat its errors. This could easily be applied to the church music/worship leader. After all, it's just your future ministry and the future happiness of your family that's at risk.

Robert Gay

Robert Gay is president and founder of Prophetic Praise Ministries and pastor of High Praise Worship Center in Panama City, Florida. He has been in full-time ministry for 17 years.

A gifted song writer, Robert has been an exclusive song writer for Integrity's Hosanna! Music. He has written many popular songs such as "No Other Name," "I Praise Your Majesty," and "On Bended Knee." Besides his own seven music recordings, Robert also led worship on Integrity's "Victor's Crown."

Traveling and teaching extensively, Robert's emphasis is on strong militant praise and imparting prophetically in both local church bodies and large regional conferences. He has authored a book on the subject of spiritual warfare through praise and worship, "Silencing the Enemy," published by Creation House Publishers. Robert has a vision to produce quality resource materials that will bring the Church out of a position of passivity into that of a militant army that will go forth and subdue all things.

Robert, his wife, Stacey, and their three children, Joshua, Kayla and Micah, live in Panama City, Florida.

The Prophetic Song

———⌘———

It seems as though every worship service is a new adventure to some degree or another. Things happen unexpectedly, sometimes things you may have never encountered before. In 1987, I went on staff as the music minister at Christian International Ministries. The ministry conducted a prophetic conference every six weeks. One of the focuses of the conferences was activating the gifts of the Holy Spirit (1 Corinthians 12:1-11; 14:1-40) in the lives of believers. As a result, there was much opportunity given in the midst of worship for people to try their wings in the prophetic song.

During one conference several people lined up to share in spontaneous prophetic song. At one point a brother began to sing. He kept singing. And singing. He would have been a great advertisement for the Energizer battery. As he continued to sing the anointing began to diminish. As the one in charge at this point, I knew it was my responsibility to do something. The next time he paused to take a breath, I jumped in and began to sing, "Everybody lift your hands and praise the Lord" and I simply kept on singing. The service was brought back on track and the people began to focus on and worship the Lord again.

Since that time I have taught on the prophetic song (often referred to as the song of the Lord) throughout the

United States and have shared this story often. There is a principle that can be learned from this story: many people, in a moment of inspiration, can get carried away. We must learn to follow what we believe the Holy Spirit is speaking, but at the same time we must recognize that there are spiritual boundaries. The prophetic song should not put a damper on the service but rather take it forward. There are several different principles that I have found helpful in the area of spontaneous prophetic songs.

The first principle is that these songs should be thematic, that is, there should be one central theme to the song. I was in a church one time where a brother began to sing spontaneously and he sang about almost every character in the Bible. At the end of his song I scratched my head wondering what he was singing about other than giving us a thorough run-down of nearly every different biblical character. We know that God is not the author of confusion, so we should not be wondering what God was trying to say after someone is finished singing a prophetic song.

Second, the song should be brief. Although there may be some rare exceptions, my experience has been that anytime someone goes for more than five minutes, they end up unnecessarily repeating themselves over and over.

The third principle I have found helpful is that the singer should sing in a normal vocal range. In one conference where I was leading worship, a sister who had formal operatic voice training began to sing a spontaneous prophetic song. She was in the vocal stratosphere where it seemed as though glass should be shattering. Although it was beautiful to hear, no one could understand what she was singing because it was so unusual to hear someone sing that high. The sister singing was very gifted in the prophetic ministry and normally declared the word of the Lord with great accuracy. But unfortunately, no one was edified at that particular moment. We were serenaded, but not built up.

Besides singing in a normal range it is imperative that the singer enunciate clearly. We desire to have the prophetic *song* not the prophetic *tune.* The purpose of the song is to communicate a message. If it can't be understood, then nothing will be communicated other than frustration in those attempting to hear.

Finally, the prophetic song should not change the direction of the service. During one particular service we were moving in a specific direction. There were even several prophetic songs that had clearly confirmed the direction in which God was leading us. It was very intense. In the midst of this, a young lady in the congregation began to sing a spontaneous song that was not in the flow of the what was going on. What she had done was out of order. What she sang was not bad nor unscriptural; it was simply brought forth at the wrong time. After she finished, we took up right where we had left off before she sang. It should be noted that the only person who should change the direction of the service is the pastor or the person that he has placed in charge of a particular aspect of the service.

At one time in my life, I felt that such specific boundaries like I have shared here would quench the Holy Spirit. I've learned that the Spirit of God is not as fragile as many people have often thought. In many of the situations I described, I could have allowed this to quench what the Lord was doing thereby causing the service to be derailed. However, one person "missing it" does not mean that the Holy Spirit flew away. The Spirit of God is ever present within us, regardless of what someone else does. A worship service can continue and achieve the purpose of God regardless of what someone in ignorance or immaturity does.

Gary Sadler

Gary Sadler is a song writer and musician called to encourage authentic, wholehearted worship in the Body of Christ. A prolific writer, he has penned many well-known worship songs (over 90 recorded on Integrity Music projects alone), and continues his quest for fresh, passionate expressions of praise to God for our day. Some of his songs include "Ancient of Days," "I Rejoice in Your Love," "He Will Come and Save You" and "Wind of God." He was also the worship leader on the Hosanna! Music recording, "King of the Ages." Along with his writing, singing and producing, Gary also leads worship and teaches at various worship conferences and seminars.

Gary enjoys all kinds of outdoor activities including mountain climbing, rappeling, hiking, mountain biking, cross country skiing and fly fishing. He lives in Franklin, Tennessee, with his wife, Debra, and their two teenage daughters, Leah and Sarah, and their Wyoming cow dog, Sam.

Worship in the Hard Places

So there I was. Banished from paradise (Jackson, Wyoming) and living in an area I had referenced on numerous occasions to be the one place I would never live. And it pressed in on me like heavy-duty pliers. The pace of a very driven city (you can see it in their eyes on the highway). The death of my parents. A threatening lawsuit. Confusing crossroads. Sickness. Intricate complications that Agatha Christie couldn't have thought up. And worse, far worse. We drove up and there was a big "No Peace" sign out front. We saw it everywhere we went, throughout the entire city, in every store, in every restaurant, church and home, worn like a sticker on a hat by every person we met. "No Peace, not here, not for you." You might be asking right now, "What has this got to do with relating a significant, insightful event in a worship setting?" Everything!

It's just that I knew so much. I knew that worship had actually very little to do with music, that our true worship was a life simply given to God, lived out for His glory and purposes. I knew how to write worship songs. I knew His favor, and I knew His peace. I had even developed a well-received teaching called "Warfare from the Place of Peace." Peace was within me, running through the deepest parts of me, and I and my family danced within its walls of protection for years. Peace was what I was "all about." Nothing was going to take my peace away...

But where was my peace now? How had it been stripped from me so quickly and so thoroughly? Without warning. A Pearl Harbor of the soul! I went to bed with butterflies in my stomach, only to awaken in the morning with them still flying around down there. Zeros. Still bombing me senseless. My defenses were all down. I had been utterly defeated before I could even fire a shot. Peace sank to the bottom, and settled in the mud. I remember realizing one day, "God has brought me to a hard place"(Duh!!). It was all around me, physically, spiritually and circumstantially. Yeah, that's what was going on alright. I was Lot, just being vexed in Sodom for a while. God would soon send a couple of angels to get us out of this mess. They'd see. A righteous man and his family in a proud, ambitious land! Bring down the fire! I called for the brimstone to make this town disappear from our memories. Wipe this mistake, this obvious error in sound judgment, from our slate and take us back to the wild, wide open spaces. Rescue us from this hard place, O Lord! Take us back so we can worship You. That was the cry of my heart.

It was after about a year of this that the night sessions began. You know, those times when you're wakened out of a sound sleep to find the Spirit of God speaking to you. You are both glad about it and terrified at the same time. What He says goes straight into your being, without hindrance, without rational opposition. So lying there, God says, "Worship me in this place." That same thing I had heard Him say twice in Jackson (Wyoming). It was so easy then out there. But this was now, and it was here, in Nashville, which I had come to view as a sort of Purgatory, only worse.

He would speak, and I would remember... How I used to love to draw near to Him all by myself. How my heart would find the wind and the water and the wild, open places, the ranges in which I found room to run free. That place had always been in Him. The best thing in my life had been His presence, and it had been so long since I had gone there. I found myself reeling from the realization that the hard place wasn't in the terrible times or circumstances. The hard place wasn't in Nashville. The hard place was within me!

I know, I know, I still haven't said anything about a specific worship event. But I'm not finished. It has been about another year since all of this took place. We still live in the Nashville area. We still have reservations about calling it home, because it still doesn't feel like home. Not yet. Life isn't perfect, or even what it used to be. But God is here. And we worship Him here in this place. He is doing new and wonderful things, breaking old boxes and starting fresh fires. In finding that truth, our perspectives have been altered.

I heard Rick Pitino, head coach of the Boston Celtics, say recently that he has two choices when he gets out of bed each day. He can be depressed and wonder why he was so crazy to have left such a cushy job at the University of Kentucky, with a winning basketball program, with all of its perks, or he can be grateful for the opportunity to meet yet another challenge head on, to restore the legendary Celtics program to championship form, and just see what happens. It is all perspective for him. His perception of what life holds for him makes the difference.

Well, God has a vision for us—a picture of all we are to be in Him. He knows what it takes to break us, to mold us, to change us. I have begun to see the challenges as an extension of His mercy to me and my family—an opportunity to live on the edge, and see what happens. Who wants to go to their grave bored to death anyway? So we have chosen to have an adventure. We now see (along with many other worshipers here) that God wants to make a move in this town that will affect all the nations. He wants to influence the influencers. He wants to do such a new thing, kindle such a hot flame, that the little religious people within us all are annihilated, consumed by the revealed glory of a furiously zealous God. I love that God is doing the "things that we did not expect" (Isaiah 64:3). I love that He is blasting out of the theological cave we placed Him in.

So, what does all this have to do with a worship event in my life? As I said before, everything. What He has done in my heart the last two years has affected everything in my life. This includes my expression of worship and the awareness of His presence and favor in those specific times. He reminds me that for any worship event to be real or significant, there must be something real and significant going on in the real world of our lives. He makes me recall that our songs merely reflect and express Who He is and what He is doing, and simply provide an environment for Him to do it even more. In my worship times, I am made very aware of how He has shown His loving kindness to me, and it humbles me. He has changed me. He is not finished, of course (I would hate to be left like this), but He has been pounding away day and night. There is a fire in me that has never burned before. Not this fire. There is an eagerness to be changed and to believe that He *will* do the impossible in our land, in our day. He is getting us ready for His next, great move. New wine demands new bottles.

I now know that He brought me to a hard place to show me the bitterness, the fear, the sin that was there, inside of me. He's doing a work He could have never done within the comfortable realm of paradise. He is sending the wind and the water to me. I run free in the wild, open places. I am living in the place of peace once again. That place is in Him.

Frank Hernandez

As a worship leader, song writer, and producer, Frank Hernandez has been involved in Christian music ministry for over 25 years. He began with the Agape Force, an evangelistic ministry that did many inner-city outreaches. That outreach to children eventually led to the creation of the music group, Candle, which recorded such award-winning albums as the platinum-selling "The Music Machine" and the gold-certified "Bullfrogs and Butterflies."

In 1979, Frank and his wife, Betsy, were married and shortly thereafter helped form the popular contemporary group, Silverwind. For Silverwind's first recording Frank wrote the well-known worship chorus, "I Will Bless the Lord."

After Silverwind, Frank's creative input continued on projects including, "The Bible: The Amazing Book," "Pleasant Dreams," created for Worlds of Wonder and "Little Clowns of Happytown," a Saturday-morning series for the ABC Television Network.

Residing in Nashville, Tennessee, with Betsy and their two children since 1989, Frank now writes and produces for the EMI Christian Music Group. He and Betsy have created several more children's CDs and video series including "Hide 'Em in Your Heart" and "The Adventures of Prayer Bear," both featuring Sparrow music artist, Steve Green.

Since 1993, he has been actively involved in his church, New Song Christian Fellowship in children's ministry as pastor, choir director, and worship leader.

Dominos

For some years it has been my privilege to lead children in worship each Sunday morning at our church, New Song Christian Fellowship, in Brentwood, Tennessee. For a time I was also the Kid's Choir Director. As many churches do, each year our Kid's Choir would usually rehearse for and perform a musical production during the Christmas and spring seasons.

This past year, however, we decided to do something entirely different. We wanted to give our children a special opportunity to lead the grownups in worship during a Sunday morning service. Each week for two months we had various worship leaders come in and teach the children about worship and the difference between performing and ministering. We learned new songs of praise and of course, we worshiped! The children grew more and more excited as they realized that though they were young, their spirits were as big as any adult's. I, too, gained a deeper appreciation of Psalm 8:2, "From the lips of children and infants You have ordained praise..."

The week before we were to lead in the Sunday morning service, the children wanted to do one last thing in preparation, something many of them had never done before. We all decided to fast for at least one day. Our choir at that time was made up of about 50 children between first and sixth grade. Obviously, then, many of them were too young to go without food for a whole day. Because of this, some of them fasted one meal, others gave up television or video games and more than one, not entirely understanding the spirit of sacrifice, volunteered to give up school. But everyone prayed and earnestly believed that the Spirit of God would minister powerfully on Sunday morning.

It was a wonderful service. The children raised their voices and lifted their hands in praise and the congregation followed. During one of the songs, several children spoke into the microphone giving thanks to God for their moms and dads, for their dogs and cats, for yummy food to eat, for a house to live in and, of course, for Jesus dying on the cross. These prayers of thanks were so simple but from pure hearts. There wasn't a dry eye in the place.

When the worship time had concluded, all the children were gathered in the choir room to talk about what the Lord had done and to thank Him again. They were very excited and talking about "dominos."

"Pizza?" I thought. "How could they be thinking of food at a time like this?"

And then they told me. During the service as we had begun leading a song called "Come Let Us Bow Down and Worship," my back had been turned to the congregation. What I did not see was, starting with the first row and continuing to the back of the church, the people had spontaneously fallen to their knees in worship. I had seen them standing one minute and on their knees the next, but to the children it looked as though the Spirit of God had touched the front row and down went the rest, like a giant set of dominos!

That morning, through the children and in them, I experienced worship as I never had before. It was an experience I will not soon forget.

Kirk and Deby Dearman

Few song writers reach in a lifetime the pinnacle of praise and worship recognition that Kirk and Deby Dearman have achieved in one song. "We Bring the Sacrifice of Praise" is sung in virtually every language and is consistently listed in Christian Copyright Licensing International's top 10 songs sung by the church universally. Kirk and Deby have traveled extensively throughout North America, Great Britain and the continent of Europe for over 15 years and are currently ministers of worship and the arts at Christ Episcopal Church in Mobile, Alabama.

Deby has turned a long-time hobby, photography, into a second income. She has had several photos published and shot album covers during their time in Nashville. They both enjoy spending time at the beach and find it very rejuvenating.

Kirk and Deby have been married for 25 years. They have two daughters, Liberty and Kristen, and one grandson, Elijah.

Make His Praise Glorious

In 1984 our family moved to Europe. We joined long-time friends, Jim and Anne Mills, in the ancient city of Augsburg, Germany. Many weeks were given to prayer and worship as we listened together for the voice of God to clarify our call. Our mission as songwriters and worship leaders became clear: we were to make His praise glorious (Psalm 66:2). The overtitle of our ministry became "Demonstrating Praise to the Nations" and our touring company was called "Project Exalt!"

While meditating on the Scripture "make His praise glorious," our spirits began to soar as we envisioned creative worship services incorporating the arts. We pictured candlelight processions, worshipers bowing at the altars of beautiful cathedrals, dancers kneeling in prayer and laying prostrate before the cross, true expressions of lives yielded to the Savior. We longed to share not only through song lyrics, but also through actual worshipers expressing through movement what the lyrics proclaimed.

We quickly found that our frustrations in sharing the gospel verbally were overcome by adding the visual arts to worship. Our praise enhanced by visual expression seemed to bypass the intellect and go straight to the heart. Worship music and sacred dance choreographed together as an expression of our faith became our new method of ministry. Hopes and dreams of leading Europeans into the presence of God were realized in the form of a worship musical entitled "Canticum ad Deum," Latin for "Song Unto God."

We enlisted an international team of musicians and dancers, all of whom were young Christians excited about using their gifts and talents for the Lord. We wrote songs and translated them into German. After an intensive training time, we began our tour throughout Europe.

Looking back on our ministry in Europe, we realize that the arts, when combined with worship, are more powerful than we had ever imagined. Hard hearts melted and stone faces softened as dancers beautifully expressed their hearts and exalted Jesus. With graceful movements, trained dancers bypassed language and intellectual barriers. The art form itself spoke volumes!

Visual images became sermons we could never find words to express. The songs were simple and led the way into the holy of holies. Our audience sensed the tangible presence of God, many for the first time in their lives.

Symbol played an important role in our worship experience as well. Magnificent cathedrals provided a sacred space already dedicated to the glory of God. Complete with brilliant stained glass windows, intricate mosaics and inspiring frescos, the very ground we stood on reflected God's glory. The bread, cup, Bible, Cross, and candles carried down the aisle in procession prepared the audience for the message. They were people desperate for hope and a faith they could see, touch and feel. Not only did they hear, but they vividly saw the message. Now they had sacred symbols from which to draw inspiration to enter into God's presence themselves.

Project Exalt! continued for several years as we ministered in cathedrals with worship teams. The ministry, now called Creative Arts Europe, is still flourishing. Led by Jim and Anne Mills, it is based at The Arts House in Brussels, Belgium.

As we returned to the States in 1991 we began to experience a void in corporate worship. In the midst of culture shock and re-entry, we would go to church desperately needing time to sit quietly in God's presence and be washed from the stress and strain of life. Often we would go home disappointed. It seemed that too many worship times were loud, hyped or sometimes cut short if a silent moment occurred. Something deep within us yearned for time to linger in the Lord's presence. We needed time to heal from the storms that so often surrounded us.

When we were invited to start a monthly worship service at St. Matthias Episcopal Church in Nashville, Tennessee, we realized that God was giving us the opportunity to birth a uniquely different kind of worship service that might meet the needs we were feeling. As we waited in listening prayer, God spoke and the vision became clear—a service of worship incorporating the arts!

We decided to name this service "Come to the Quiet." We began to build on the foundation that had been laid in the cathedrals of Europe.

Symbol had become so important to us. We longed once again to experience the beauty of symbol we had found in the cathedrals. As we allowed God to shape our vision, we felt that He wanted us to incorporate the use of candlelight, ringing bells, interpretive reading of the Scripture, processions, music and responsive readings around a particular theme. Sensing that the Church was longing to re-connect with its historical roots, we began to study church history and set various ancient creeds and prayers to music.

As worship leaders now at Christ Episcopal Church in Mobile, Alabama, we have introduced "Come to the Quiet" as a regular ministry. It has been so exciting to see the artists of our church come alive as their gifts are utilized in worship: visual arts, carpenters, painters, songwriters, script writers, readers, sound and light technicians, musicians, actors, dancers—all worshiping the Lord with their gifts. Our church now sees this service as an outreach to the community, as it draws many who would never come to a typical Sunday service.

As we move into the 21st century, our methods of communicating the gospel must be relevant to the times and to our culture. We live in a visually-oriented society and we are daily bombarded with ungodly symbols and imagery. I believe God wants to restore symbol and imagery to His Church.

Each of us as worship leaders have a unique call. It is vital that we spend time in the Lord's presence listening before we lead. His ideas are so far above anything we could create on our own. If we don't listen, how will we discover the unique way He has called us to present IIis word and lead people into His presence?

Lindell Cooley

Raised a preacher's kid, Lindell Cooley had seen all that religion had to offer...and he wasn't impressed. However, he had witnessed the reality of God and his spirit responded to God's call at an early age.

A self-taught musician, Lindell's talents improved and matured with hard work, encouragement from friends, and on-the-job-training at his dad's church.

At the age of 14, Lindell felt the Lord tell him that he would be used to take music around the world. Despite the seeming impossibility of such a thought, the strong sense of destiny to that end never departed. Lindell became an accomplished musician with many accolades to his credit, but it was nearly 20 years before God plucked him from obscurity and placed him at Brownsville Assembly in Pensacola, Florida. He has been the music minister at Brownsville since the spring of 1995.

In 1997, Lindell founded Music Missions International, a ministry to spread the gospel of Jesus to the world through ministry, music and missions endeavors.

Lindell, his wife, Amber, and their son, Samuel, live in Pensacola, Florida.

The Night the Angels Sang

Adapted from the book, *A Touch of Glory*
(published by Revival Press, 1997)

Very early in the revival at our church we noticed supernatural occurrences in the worship service that let us know God was personally involved in this revival, even in areas not related to the hundreds of souls won each night. I looked in my personal journal and found an entry dated August 17, 1995 (about two months after the revival began). This is what happened that night:

The service tonight seemed to be pretty average until the very end. As I was about to leave, I talked with Richard Crisco, the youth pastor, and he questioned me about a particular worship chorus we sang toward the end of the service. It was an ad lib thing that we had sung spontaneously. He wanted to know how I was able to cue the sound track tape to come in as precisely as it did. I told him there was no tape, it was just me and the keyboard—there weren't even any singers. When I explained this to him, he didn't believe me. He said that he had heard at least three voices and several instruments.

As Richard spoke, I remembered that I too had heard another voice singing a beautiful counter melody, but was so caught up in worshiping the Lord that I didn't see who was singing. I knew I was singing, and I assumed it was Jeff

Oettle (one of the worship singers at the time), or someone else who had grabbed the microphone to join in.

As Richard talked, I remembered hearing a backup voice and a third voice come in that was singing a perfect counter melody to my song. The third voice was exceptionally clear, and the counter melody sounded rehearsed. That should have been impossible, since I was making it up as I went along. Yet, this voice was singing a perfect counter melody with amazing clarity at the same time I was singing.

Later on, Bennie Johnson (the sound engineer) and Vann Lane (the children's pastor) told me they had heard it too. They were at the sound board, and were trying to find out what channel the third voice was on. (It wasn't coming through the sound board at all!)

Later that week I asked Jeff Oettle, "Were you singing with me?"

"No, but I was standing on stage."

Then I asked him, "Did anybody else sing with me?"

I already knew the answer. "No."

My conclusion was that the voice was definitely not of this world.

Two girls from Puerto Rico who had backgrounds in witchcraft came to the revival that night. When I started singing this song, hundreds of people were still being prayed for at the altars. Normally it is pretty loud. However, as this song began, accompanied only by the keyboard, everything became totally quiet. The song (with the heavenly voices) was so impressive that everyone stopped to listen. (Everybody I questioned that night heard it.) This went on for probably two or three minutes.

When I stopped singing, one of the Puerto Rican girls sitting to my far right released a blood-curdling scream, and I thought, "How rude of you to interrupt." But it was as though a demon had left. The girl told one of the intercessors who was working with her that she had tried to get deliverance from the witchcraft that she had practiced for years, and she'd never been really free of it. Once the angels started singing, that demon left her, and she was totally free.

John R. Throop

Dr. John R. Throop's interest in and love of worship began with his Roman Catholic upbringing in Evanston, Illinois. Since then, he has found his spiritual home in the Episcopal Church and was ordained a priest in 1981. He has served several churches in Illinois and Ohio, and currently is vicar of Christ Church, Limestone (near Peoria, Illinois), leading worship in a historic stone building built in 1845.

For over 12 years, John has worked for spiritual revival and worship renewal in the Episcopal Church, coordinating the 3Rs Conference in Florida in 1986 and becoming the first executive director of Episcopalians United for Revelation, Renewal and Reformation in 1987.

In 1995, he earned his doctorate in organizational development and renewal from Fuller Theological Seminary and has formed a management consulting practice, The Summit Group, which works with companies and nonprofit organizations on strategic planning and organizational development issues. He also works with churches on renewal and planning issues, and he is in demand as a retreat conductor. He is a frequently published writer, with articles in Worship Leader, Leadership, and The Clergy Journal, and *other national and international publications and devotional guides. He and his wife, Cindy Ford, live in Peoria, and he has two children, Sarah and Emilie.*

Worship in the Moment of Truth

It's one thing to prepare in seminary to lead worship on Sundays. Early in my ministry, I found that it's quite another to lead worship at a funeral.

Learning about worship didn't prepare me for the stark reality of death, standing before a casket, grieving family in front of me, leading a funeral and groping for the most comforting thing to say and the most appropriate prayer to pray. Here, people ache to hear the truth: "Death has been swallowed up in victory!"

One of the most important lessons funerals have taught me is the constant effort I must make as a worship leader to balance the transcendent and the immanent. I have wrestled in these services to keep the focus on Christ while maintaining a warm, personal and intimate touch at a time when nearly everyone in attendance is vulnerable and tender. What's more, if there ever were seeker services, funerals are the prime moments when people who have never learned about worship and who perhaps have not set foot in a church for years (if ever) are present and open.

Not long after finishing seminary and entering the ordained ministry, I was asked to officiate at a funeral of a man in his late 40s who had committed suicide. Residents of my community, neither he nor his wife had been active in the life of a church in years, and only God could know the state of his heart. I had never met them. A friend of the wife who was active in another church in my denomination called and asked if I would conduct the service in the church. I agreed to do it.

Later that afternoon, I met with the new widow in the very living room where her husband had shot himself and where she had discovered him when she came home from work. Blood still stained the carpet and the unmistakable stench of death still filled the house, even though her husband's body had been removed hours earlier. There was a heaviness and despair in the room as we met, and I prayed for the light of Christ to illumine the darkness and the sadness. I knew enough then about spiritual warfare to determine that we definitely could not make plans for worship at a funeral of a suicide victim without the presence of Christ.

Frankly, I couldn't think of anything to say. It was a moment when the Spirit gave me the words to speak.

Tearfully and humbly, the woman began to speak of the horror of finding her husband dead on the floor, his depression finally overcoming him. She spoke of her absence from the church and her reluctance to come to me, feeling as if she were imposing on me. She had no idea where to begin or how the service should be conducted, only hoping that the service would not be filled with guilt and blame, and that her friend could sing.

The pastoral needs were evident. This funeral could be a time of warm embrace or a cold comfort to this woman. The worship task was formidable. How could God be praised at the funeral of a man who had snuffed out his own life? No course in seminary had prepared me for this dilemma so early in my ministry. In the 16 years since then, the challenge is no less daunting in the funerals where I officiate.

There was one other complication. The church was in the process of being renovated, and the carpet layers were scheduled to do their work the day of the funeral.

I put three lessons to work in planning for this time of worship. First, I understood that the sorrow and horror of the man's death could be countered only by a stirring affirmation of God the Father, the author of life and the giver of hope. It was important to worship, not just to gather. Secondly, I did not give a eulogy, but preached the Gospel. A eulogy focuses much more on the person and his or her life, and much less on what God is doing or saying through the person's death. Finally, I realized the importance of a sermon which articulates the questions people have in the hearts—which are many, at any funeral (much less a tragic one such as this). The prayers and the worship must lead those present to begin to find their answers in Christ.

The day came for the funeral, and we literally rolled out the red carpet for the entrance of the casket. As I began the service, even with a wonderful pastoral resource such as the Episcopal Book of Common Prayer, it was important to welcome people to the service and explain very gently and briefly what would be taking place and what we as a congregation would be doing. God is here, I said, and He wants us to come into His presence just as we are. I have introduced nearly every funeral since then with such a greeting, which helps to place the unchurched as well as the churched at ease.

In the sermon, I articulated some questions. Does God love the deceased? What is the hope available to us that seemed to elude him? What is God saying to us through this man's death? What is eternal life, and is it available to us? What will we do now because we have been in this place today? I let the Scriptures speak.

The singing friend also used a Roman Catholic worship song, "On Eagle's Wings," to help people to focus their grief and their hope, and to participate in worship rather than sit as sad spectators. Those attending commented later on the power of the music to channel their feelings and direct their thoughts. Many who participated said that the service was the "best" funeral they had ever attended because they were able to leave thinking of their own need of God, and with some hope, not only for their friend, but for themselves.

In seminary, I do not recall in worship or pastoral care classes exactly how one ought to lead a funeral service, and how worship and grief are related. This was a lesson I learned from a senior pastor who was an excellent mentor, from reflecting prayerfully on my own worship experiences in funerals, and by attending other funerals which were anything but worship.

Since this turning point, I have found many funerals to be times of profound worship, times when God is palpably present in the midst of sadness and suffering. In some cases, the worship has enabled participants to celebrate God's presence and power in the person's life and death. Funerals are unique in their highlight of our mortality and the promise of eternal life to those who believe, and the truth of the Gospel to those who do not. For at the gate of death, we are closer to God than at any time. Thoughtful, well-planned worship in funerals reaches for His nearness.

Tom Kraeuter

Tom Kraeuter is a gifted communicator who has been face-to-face with thousands of believers from all walks of the Body of Christ. People of all ages receive new insights from his straight-forward, humorous style.

Tom regularly ministers in Bible-believing churches of all types. From Assemblies of God to Presbyterian, Baptist to Pentecostal, Vineyard to Mennonite, the response is always overwhelmingly positive.

As an author, Tom has seven books to his credit including "Keys to Becoming an Effective Worship Leader" and "The Worship Leader's Handbook," available in bookstores worldwide. He is the former managing editor of Psalmist magazine and his writings have appeared in nationally-recognized periodicals.

Some of Tom's other favorite activities include reading to his children, cooking, playing table tennis and eating chocolate.

Since 1984, Tom Kraeuter (pronounced Kroyter) has been a part of the leadership team of Christian Outreach Church, near St. Louis, Missouri. He and his wife, Barbara, and their three children, David, Stephen and Amy, reside in Hillsboro, Missouri.

The Deadly Disease of...Perfectionism

"What's the matter with you?" my wife asked.

"Nothing."

"Excuse me, but I know you better than that. Now, what's wrong?"

"Okay, okay," I responded. "Everything went wrong in the service this morning."

"*Everything* went wrong? I can't remember *anything* being wrong."

"Where were you? The transition between 'Holy, Holy, Holy' and 'Blessed Be the Lord God Almighty' was awful. The drummer missed the endings of two songs. And our monitors were not working at all when we went back up after the sermon. The whole service was a catastrophe!"

My wife smiled. "Let me get this straight," she replied. "All but one transition went well, the drummer did great except for the ending of two songs, and the monitors worked well except for the closing song. Is that correct?"

"Well.. yeah, I guess."

"So really almost everything went *right*." Her smile broadened, "Right?"

"Oh, you just don't understand."

In retrospect, I have realized that it was me who didn't understand. It took me a long time to admit it, but I suffer from a potentially deadly affliction that plagues many worship leaders: perfectionism. Statistics indicate that nearly five out of every five worship leaders have it. If you have this horrendous disease you know exactly what I'm talking about. It can sap your strength and steal your joy. If 99 things go right and one goes wrong, the only one you remember is the one that went wrong.

Services like the one described in the scenario above have been commonplace throughout my 20 years of leading worship. Of the hundreds of meetings for which I have led worship there have been perhaps only a few where everything went exactly right. The truth is that many worship leaders have told me they have never had even *one* service where everything went just right (and I thought *my* case of perfectionism was severe!).

I once heard well-known speaker Gary Smalley make a fascinating statement that really struck me. He said, "The number one cause of stress is unfulfilled expectations." Unfulfilled expectations. Like when the back-up singers go off-key. Or when the bass guitar is causing a buzz in the sound system. Our expectations are that everything will go perfectly. And when they don't they obvious result is exactly what Smalley said: stress.

Let's be realistic. As long as we live in this world, as long as we deal with people, there will always be problems. There will always be mistakes. Everything will not go perfectly. The sooner we realize this the sooner we will begin to overcome the perfectionism affliction.

I am not advocating that we stop doing our best. God is worthy of the very best we can give. However, "He knows how we are formed, He remembers that we are dust" (Psalm 103:14). God knows that we will make mistakes and those around us will make mistakes. Fortunately, that's where His grace comes in. When the level of perfection that we expect doesn't happen, His grace is still sufficient.

Over the years I have been amazed at what God has done through services that were seemingly riddled with errors. When we did most things wrong, the Lord still, like the people said of Jesus in Mark 7:37, "has done all things well."

In spite of us God is always faithful. Recognizing the fulness of His faithfulness and grace has helped me to start to live beyond the perfectionism syndrome. I still always endeavor to put forth the best possible effort, but the results are His responsibility. And if I am tempted to think that "everything went wrong" I simply trust His grace.

Daniel Jacobi

For about seven years Daniel Jacobi has been ministering as a song writer and worship leader at Christ for the Nations in Germany. His desire is to mobilize the young generation of his nation to live radically for Jesus. He wants to see thousands of teens being saved through evangelistic praise and worship.

Daniel is married to Annette. Together with their three children, David, Josia and Esther, they reside in Bad Gandersheim, Germany.

Learning to Walk

One of the important lessons I learned about leading worship was one that God didn't reveal to me in class or at any worship seminar, but at home through my oldest son, David. The Bible teaches us that we have to come to God like little children to enter the kingdom of God (Matthew 18:3). I have found this to be true for worship leaders also.

I remember the days when David was still a baby. As a father I was proud of him when he began to walk. It was such a pleasure for me to see him taking a step or two. More times than not, however, those first steps turned into falls. David would fall down and frequently bump his head causing him to cry—but only for a moment. Just as quickly, he was back on his feet trying it again. With a lot of tenacity he was finally not only walking but running around our house.

After many struggles and failures of my own, I finally realized that our Father in heaven sees worship leaders the same way. When we are just beginning, God doesn't expect us to be full-grown, mature worship leaders. He is very aware that we need to learn and grow in leading worship. I believe He even enjoys every little step forward we make. It is easy to miss this lesson. I almost did. I was often so tense and worried about myself that I missed the joy of learning.

When I started to lead worship here in Glaubens-Zentrum (the German branch of Christ for the Nations Bible Institute in Dallas, Texas), I was often devastated when I chose an inappropriate song or when I started in the wrong key. I still remember one day when I tried to motivate a bunch of wild teenagers to rejoice before the Lord. I did my best to find the most up-beat songs, but all I got was a tired yawning. These times (which every worship leader goes through) were terribly humiliating for me. So much so, that everybody in the school knew that when I made a mistake in one worship service, the next one would usually be worse just because of my fear of failing again.

However, while my son David was learning to walk, he never once was embarrassed or devastated when he fell to the floor. He simply stood back up and tried it again. And again. And again. I'm sure that all totaled it was literally hundreds of times that he fell and got up. During this process he learned how to do it better and better. Please realize that this does not mean he will never fall again. (In fact, just last week *I* fell and hurt my ankle.) However, even when he does fall he does not just lay there and refuse to move; he doesn't give up.

When I realized that, the truth of it hit me right between the eyes. It was such a great release for me to realize that my Father in heaven, Whom I long to worship with all of my heart, even supports me through my struggles and failures as a worship leader. I am His child, and He will never leave me or forsake me. He already sees in me a boy who walks perfectly.

Chris Falson

Chris Falson is originally from Australia and now resides in California. He has been leading worship since 1987 and was the worship pastor for a large church in Australia until 1993. Since then he has been sent out as a worship missionary to countries all over the world. He has produced records for a number of labels including Maranatha! Music. He was a member of the Maranatha Promise Keeper Band from 1993-97, leading worship for thousands of men in stadiums across America.

Chris is also the composer of such songs as "I See the Lord," "All Honor" and "Walk by Faith."

Chris, his wife and their two sons live in Los Angeles.

Reluctant Leaders Can Make Fruitful Trees
Adapted from the book,
Planted by the Water, The Making of a Worship Leader
(published by The Orchard, 1998)

On his way to London to pursue further ministry aspirations, my predecessor threw me the keys to my new office and wished me luck. No last minute advice, no tips for success and no working manual on how to be a music director or worship leader.

Apart from leading the band on Sundays, I really did not know what was required of me. I was naive enough to think that I would have plenty of spare time on my hands.

I was very nervous about filling the shoes of my departing and very successful leader. Although I was a worshiper, I didn't think I could actually lead a congregation in worship. I had been a reliable member of the worship team, but I had no idea on how to build and nurture a eam of singers, musicians and sound engineers. I had written and arranged music for clubs and theater shows, but that did not mean I knew how to write a good worship song.

Whereas others may have deemed themselves perfect for the job, I did not know where to start. Though a professional musician for many years in the mainstream world of music, I knew I was walking into uncharted territory. My whole being cried out, "I can't do this!"

I do not know about you, but I draw considerable comfort from the fact that most of the great men and women of the Bible were also reluctant leaders. However, they were called by God out of the wilderness and fulfilled assignments that seemed beyond them.

Consider Noah. God recognized him as a righteous man and so confided in him the plan to flood the earth and wipe out all that was evil. In doing so, God gave Noah instructions on how to build a boat that would save him and his family from death. Bible scholars tell us that until this time the earth had never experienced rain since it was covered by a watery mist. The test for Noah was to build the ark in the sight of all his peers who naturally would have ridiculed and taunted him day and night. What could he have said to convince them of his purpose? Nothing. He merely had to obey and trust God to lead him over the waters and on to dry land.

In a similar manner, Abraham defied the natural laws of age to father two nations. Joseph, sold into slavery, trusted God to turn evil into good. He was elevated from the prison cell to the most powerful seat in Egypt. David, a forgotten shepherd boy, was prepared by God out in the fields to restore Israel as a worshiping nation.

Rahab, Esther, Daniel, Mary, Peter and Paul are all admired today as men and women of faith, yet they all felt inadequate and under-qualified for what God had called them to do. Somehow, each trusted God and became history makers in the process.

If you are nervous about taking on a leadership position or lack self-assurance for what you see ahead, you may be just the person to whom God is looking.

In my mind there have always been people with more skill, charisma, experience, maturity and all-around qualifications for the position of worship leader than me. So why would God ask me to be a leader? We read the Lord's words to Samuel: "Do not consider his appearance or his height, for I have rejected him. The Lord does not look at the things man looks at. Man looks at the outward appearance but the Lord looks at the heart" (1 Samuel 16:7).

For me, the deciding factor for taking the job as worship leader was my pastor's confidence in me. He was and still is above all things to me a worshiper, and he considered me worthy to become a worship leader. This was enough encouragement for me to take a step of faith and say, "I'm willing if you are, Lord." I will always be grateful for His leading me in this direction.

From there, I had to follow Noah's steps: obey and trust. Fortunately, God had provided a book of instructions to help me along the way. Joshua 1:8 promises that if we meditate on God's law day and night, we will find success and prosperity. Meditating on the words of Jeremiah 17, I discovered that my lack of confidence in myself allowed for confidence in God's ability to move on my behalf. "Blessed is he that trusts in the Lord, whose confidence is in Him. He will be like a tree planted by the water that sends out its roots to the stream. It does not fear when heat comes; its leaves are always green. It has no worries in a year of drought and never fails to bear fruit" (Jeremiah 17:7-8).

The immediate challenge was to be patient and still, like the tree planted by the water. During the first month of my tenure, I began each day by speaking this Scripture over my life. Within a few days, I knew it by heart and no matter where I was or what I was doing I'd remind myself that I was just like that tree planted by the water.

One day while praying, it was like coming out of a dark room into sunshine. I realized that I was extremely blessed, unbelievably blessed in fact, for I actually had confidence in the Lord to work through me. My confidence did not have to be, nor was it ever meant to be, in me. Such a simple revelation changed my life forever.

Jeremiah 17:5-6 amplifies this by saying: "Cursed is the one who trusts in man...he'll be like a bush in the wastelands, he will not see prosperity when it comes."

No longer did I have to consider my lack of experience and knowledge as a detriment to my ministry, but rather an asset. It became part of the learning process that when I am weak, I am actually very strong, if I let the Lord fill the gap.

To this day, although I have learned many things and increased my storehouse of knowledge and wisdom, the Scripture about the "tree by the water" still helps me to let go and to let God fill the platform, the church building, the worship team, the congregation, my family, my finances and in fact, whatever He wants with His presence.

My greatest times of success in ministry have been the result of me getting out of God's way. No matter how small the problem, it is always too big for me to handle on my own, so I step aside (eventually) and let Him take over. Whether I am leading worship, writing a song, counseling a friend, or, like David, facing Goliath in my path, there is a recognition that He is God and I am not; that He will give grace to the humble and lift me in due time (1 Peter 4:6-7).

John Chevalier

John Chevalier is an associate pastor and the director of worship and music ministries at Desert Son Community Church in Tucson, Arizona. With over 13 years experience in worship ministry, he also founded and serves as president of Moriah Ministries, a nonprofit corporation with the goal of "equipping believers for a lifestyle of worship." He is a conference speaker and consultant in the area of worship ministry and divorce recovery ministry. His teaching and outreach, in the area of divorce recovery, has touched the lives of hundreds of individuals seeking to rebuild their lives.

He has also served as the program chairman, as well as developing and overseeing the worship and music ministry curriculum, for the San Francisco Bay Area Church Workers Convention in Castro Valley, California. He is a faculty member at the International Worship Institute in Dallas, Texas.

John's deepest desire is to know and experience the reality of God, and to communicate and encourage others to seek out that reality and experience all that God has for them. His greatest joy in ministry is to see believers truly experience God's grace and accept His unconditional forgiveness regardless of their circumstances or their past.

John, his wife, Becky, and their four children, Sarah, Timothy, Jonathan and Stephanie, live in Tucson, Arizona.

"I Am Your Father"

It was May of 1995. I found myself on a plane headed from my home, north of San Francisco, to the Northeast to visit my parents. This would be different than my other visits because this time my father lay in a hospital bed, his life slowly slipping away. I had not seen him in about five years and really didn't know what to expect when I arrived.

My older brother met me at the airport, and we immediately left for the hospital. After the initial greetings and hugs from mom, my focus turned to dad. Others in the family had prepared me for dad's condition, but there's nothing quite like being there to make reality set in. I remember my dad as always being very sharp mentally and pretty strong physically, especially for being just over five feet tall. Nothing much ever riled him, but when it did, look out! This was not the same man I remembered. It was so out of character for him to be totally unresponsive to my greeting.

Over the next week, I spent most of my time at the hospital, being with dad and supporting mom. We almost lost him on two occasions that week, but when it was time for me finally to return to my family on the West Coast, he was still with us.

I returned home with a heavy burden. Although we hadn't seen each other for years, it was as if I was about to lose the most precious person in my life. I remembered all the little things my father did for me as I grew up. The time, during a rain delay at Shea Stadium, when he found a way to get me into the bullpen to meet my favorite ballplayer. The times that he showed up, when my high school rock band would play at area dances, knowing full well that we would not be doing his favorite Frank Sinatra numbers. Memories of all the ground balls hit to me. The fishing trips off the end of our dock. The time he patiently looked for the wrench I dropped in the lake while we were working on the boat. It all came rushing back to me, as if it were yesterday.

Two months went by. I was in contact with my mother almost daily until our family vacation in July. I purposed to leave my burden at home as we traveled to visit my wife's family in Southern California. As I always seem to do while on vacation, I carved out some time to visit a fellow worship leader at his church in Los Angeles. I sat in on his worship rehearsal and enjoyed the time we had together that evening. We said our good-byes, and I left the church to return to Orange County.

On my way home, my thoughts were focused on the events of that evening and my task as a worship leader.

Then, from nowhere, I heard a voice, as though the person was in the car with me. The voice simply said, "I am your Father." The presence of God filled my Dodge Caravan like I had never felt it before. I recognized the voice of my heavenly Father speaking into my spirit as it came a second time, "I am your Father."

In tears, I focused on the Lord, wanting to hear more, but I didn't. I just knew that, for whatever reason, my God wanted me to feel His love for me in a powerful way. As I drove on, I noticed that the heaviness that I had lived with for months was gone. I had a Father. No matter how much I would miss my earthly father when he left us behind on earth, I had a heavenly Father who loved me with more love than I could ever have experienced in my life. Although I had been in pastoral ministry for years, I had no idea of the depth of my heavenly Father's love for me—at least not until the following day.

At about 2:30 in the afternoon, I was alone at my sister-in-law's house when the phone rang. It was my mother. She said the words I had feared would come for the last three months. "John, your father just passed away." I cannot tell you what we discussed after that, nor how long I was on the phone. What I can tell you is that I was once again consumed with the love of my heavenly Father who cared enough for His earthly son that He prepared me in advance for my father's passing. The only thought that was running through my mind while my mother spoke was the fact of how great a God we serve and how much He desires to be our Father. A real Father.

On that day, my relationship with Him drastically changed. I have a God who is truly a Father to me. A Man I can look up to and admire. A Father Whom, although I still blow it at times, I can obey with 100% confidence that He has my best interest in mind. I never really doubted the love of that Father. I knew the scriptures and the reassurance of His love through His Word. But, until that day, I had never experienced the genuine love that He had for me. That same love can be experienced by all of His children. The next time you read the Bible, picture yourself as a child, sitting on your Father's lap, as He reads you a bedtime story. A story from His heart. A story that cost Him His own Son. A price that He paid so He could be a Parent to us. Listen to His heart, hear His words, and be confident that the love of your Father will never cease, regardless of the circumstances of your life.

Did that effect the way I worship? What do you think?

Ready for Anything

Those of us who lead worship know the feeling we get as we leave the platform on any given Sunday morning. We pray that the people have connected with God. We also know that besides the closing song, the worship team is pretty much done for the day. Well, on most days, that is.

I remember at the beginning of my ministry there was one Sunday, when except for myself, our total pastoral staff was out of town. Our guest speaker that morning was our mission's intern, a young man who was preparing to enter the mission field. We had spoken during the week and discussed the details of the service. Since our senior pastor normally teaches for about 55 minutes, I needed to firm up an approximate time for his sermon. He told me that he normally spoke for about 30 to 45 minutes and that this Sunday would be about the same.

Now, on this particular Sunday I chose to lead without my guitar and with only one keyboard player and a couple of vocalists. In addition, the keyboard player had asked to leave during the sermon to help in her child's Sunday school class. This was acceptable, since we had 2 services each week.

Following our worship, I greeted several people while the announcements were being made, and finally, took my seat in the rear of the worship center for the message. About 15 minutes into, what I thought was the introduction, I heard him say: "...and as I close, I urge you to pray for us as we begin our mission to..."

I couldn't believe it. He walked off the platform. No prayer, no warning. I could have used a prayer, or at least some time to think about what I would do. I confidently walked up to the platform and met a congregation who was looking at me with anticipation as to what would come next. I don't think I ever felt so alone in my life. Any musical support that I had wasn't due back for at least another 15 minutes. I looked out at the people and grasped on to the only point I could remember my brother sharing. "I want you to consider one thing this morning," I said, sweating just a bit as I recited what had been shared. "I believe that God would have us do something a little different this morning." (I believed this like I had never believed anything before in my life. I just didn't know what that would be.) "I want you to take a moment and bow your head. This is something I'd like you *all* to do today. Please take a few extra moments and ask your heavenly Father to speak to you, as you respond to the challenge laid before us. Today, I feel the Lord prompting us just to sit and reflect in total silence."

I watched as the people responded and, as soon as I was confident that every eye was closed, I slowly walked down the center isle to the back door of the worship center. Upon hitting daylight on the other side of the door, I broke into a sprint in the direction of the Sunday school department. I located my keyboard player, grabbed some extra music and headed back into the worship center. We then, together, slowly walked up to the platform and entered into an extended worship set to close out the service. God met us there and ministered to us as we (or at least some of us) considered our part in winning the world for our Lord.

The moral of the story is simply this. Be ready for anything. When it comes to God's work there is no way to predict how any service or event will come off. Be flexible. Be teachable. Listen to that still small voice, no matter how small that voice might seem at the time.

David Fischer

Dr. David Fischer is the senior pastor of Living Waters Christian Fellowship in Pasadena, California, a church known for helping birth prophetic worship expressions in many nations. He has been part of the leadership of the church for over 20 years. David has personally organized and directed prophetic praise and worship conferences in 18 nations on four continents over the past 17 years.

David is also president of Living Word Bible College and the Living Word Institute of Worship, which has trained over 1800 students in Southern California since 1984.

David and his wife, Elaine, have been married for 30 years and they live in Pasadena. They have three adult children, Paul, Julie and Karen.

Cross Cultural Worship

I was looking forward to our conference in Bogota, Colombia, with great anticipation. We had experienced a glorious conference in Cali, Colombia, the year before, in 1986. Eleven hundred delegates packed out the hotel and hundreds were turned away. The church there had been interceding for months against the guerrilla warfare in Cali, which had been greatly agitating the city. We had even been warned by several pastoral friends not to go. The U.S. Embassy official who sat next to our team on the plane into Cali said, "Don't you know that Cali has been declared off-limits to all U.S. Embassy personnel? The city is technically in a state of siege." Our team was the only group from a full flight to get off, and the stewardess twice said to us, "Do you understand that this is Cali?", as if to say, "Do you really know what you are doing?" I breathed a silent prayer and headed for the conference center.

The impact of that conference was awesome. The conference leadership had hired a radio station to broadcast 30 minutes of their first meeting. The broadcasters stayed free of charge for another hour, and calls began coming into the station. "Put this on again tomorrow!" listeners requested. Over the next four days we received a total of eight hours of free air time. Both broadcasters found the Lord. One of them even declared over the air, "I was an atheist before I attended these meetings, but I discovered the joy of the Lord and now I am a believer!"

It was at that conference that we felt compelled by God to go to the capital of Colombia, Bogota, the following year and hold a conference on a larger scale. During worship in the last service in Cali, I saw a vision of little David felling Goliath with his rock and then turning his back on the giant and jumping up and down, exclaiming, "I got him! I got him!" In my spirit I was frightened and wanted to scream at David, "Finish him off before he revives! Cut off his head!" Then I watched as the giant dazedly got up and began to approach David again. We believed this vision meant that we had won a victory, but now we were to go to the "head" of the nation for worship and warfare to help finish the job!

So I approached our first conference in Bogota with tremendous anticipation. All the major charismatic churches in the city were on board, and the conference drew 2000 registered delegates, with 3500 in the evening rallies. I always look forward to working with our Worship Symposium conferences in releasing the delegates themselves in creative, prophetic worship. To accomplish this, we always encourage the delegates to bring all their own instruments and join with our worship team in spontaneous worship music. Imagine my surprise on the first afternoon to discover that our "orchestra" consisted of 50 acoustic guitars, 30 tambourines, a percussionist, two flutes and a trumpet! What were we going to do?

As we progressed through the instrumental clinic (with about 600 looking on), with the help of the Holy Spirit and the expertise of some of our team, especially Vivien Hibbert, a beautiful sound of music began to occur. To hear 50 guitars strumming the same chord progressions in unison and 30 tambourines beating as one to the same rhythm was quite exciting, and of course, very Colombian. That nation is known for its mass guitar "choirs."

We learned a valuable lesson that year. Namely, it is possible to utilize musical styles indigenous to any culture in praise and worship.

The other joy for me, as a worship leader, was to experience the Colombian "spin" on choruses picked up from the States. With their rhythms and enthusiasm, they played songs a little differently than we "norteamericanos" would have. Their arrangements beautifully reflected their Latin American setting. Even more glorious was hearing them praise God with their "own" choruses, composed by Colombians. There was no mistaking the abandonment with which they were released to worship in their own musical styles. Especially amazing to me was watching 3000 people leap up and down in unison together for twenty minutes shouting, "Cristo! Cristo! Cristo!..." as a cloud of dust rose from the floor and filled the whole building!

Armed with this experience of worship leading in the Colombian culture, we tried this same approach of trying to adapt cultural artistic expressions of worship in another nation, with much different results. This time our team was ministering in the early 1990s in a church in Lovech, Bulgaria. This church was very progressive in praise and worship. Their worship team was turning out the best Bulgarian praise tapes in the nation.

Since the purpose of our conference was to release all forms of "Davidic" or "Psalmic" worship among the delegates, our workshops included vocal and instrumental expression as well as all forms of movement found in the Hebrew and Greek words for "dance" in Scripture. This range of movement included leaping, jumping and skipping, as well as twisting and twirling, and also involved circles of dancers and processions of praise.

In all of this, we strive to be as open and as creative as possible and to be quite sensitive to what the Holy Spirit might be initiating in the services. Toward this end, we often encourage people to "break out" of traditional modes of church music and arts expression in order to experience what the Holy Spirit might be endeavoring to release in their worship.

In this particular instance, two of the workshop leaders on the Bulgarian team had formerly been nationally known rock stars and also excellent Bulgarian folk dancers. During a worship workshop, our dance leader called out to them during a time of creative movement, when the spontaneous music was fitting, "How about doing some Bulgarian folk dance steps to this music?"

A murmur of disapproval rippled through the audience of several hundred. One of the staff quickly explained to us that in Bulgarian churches, cultural folk dance forms were taboo. They had absolutely no problem with other forms of the dance in worship—leaping, skipping, twisting, twirling, praise marches and processions, etc.—but the use of Bulgarian cultural dance was viewed as "worldly."

During the last 17 years of organizing worship conferences in 16 nations on 4 continents, I have amassed a lot of memorable experiences concerning the incorporation of cultural forms of music and movement in worship. Sometimes cultural forms are totally rejected, sometimes completely accepted!

One flashback concerns a fantastic worship conference in San Jose, Costa Rica, in October of 1996 which actually featured Costa Rican "Folkorico" dancers in full national costume. They were preceded by a video presentation of the natural beauty of the nation, supplied by the Department of Tourism!

Other memories include the refusal of some Latin American churches to use the marimba in worship because of its use in *cantinas*, or bars, with "worldly" songs—a sort of "guilt by association." I couldn't help thinking of Psalm 8, which David wrote to be accompanied by a Philistine harp! (A Psalm upon "Gittith": "a Gittite harp," from "Gath, a Philistine city"—Strong's Concordance).

I also remember a statement made years ago by a fellow worship leader, when electronic instruments first began to be used in churches: "There is no "sin" in *syn*thesizer"!

Another painfully vivid memory is of a national worship conference in Bogota in the early 1990s. One pastor on our platform, who had brought 1000 of his people to the conference, buried his face in his hands during one of our choreographed worship expressions and finally had to leave the platform. We found out later that it was because we used a banner with the emblem of a lamb on it, signifying the Lord. He thought we were worshiping a "graven image"! He later told us with some degree of justification that he had been working hard to get his new converts weaned away from worship icons and statues and was trying to focus them on believing the Word of God. To him it was fine if the banners had words on them, for example, "Gloria al Cordero de Dios" ("Glory to the Lamb of God"), but definitely not symbols!

I have reached two conclusions from all of these experiences in other cultures that I like to share with other worship leaders. The first is that we need to be quite informed about and sensitive to the beliefs of the churches in which we minister concerning their inclusion or exclusion of their own cultural music and movement styles in their worship expressions to the Lord. I always follow the practice of discussing with the senior leadership of each conference the parameters for worship expression which they recommend and then try to follow them as best I can.

Secondly, after having led worship in many cultures, I am more and more convinced that the Holy Spirit desires to sanctify and bless a multitude of worship expressions. If we will give Him the freedom, He will release a greater tide of spiritual renewal and blessing into our services. I now believe that what makes music and movement "holy" or "profane" is the Spirit behind it and not the particular cultural styles of expression themselves.

We would do well in our American churches to apply "cross cultural" principles to our own worship services as well. Are we allowing a variety of expression in our services which minister to the different racial and ethnic groups within our own local congregations? And what about generational differences? Are we providing a balance between the "good old hymns" which minister to our elderly members and the hot new contemporary worship chorus which excite our youth?

Our God is a God of variety, and we are creatures of habit. He acts with an eye to the future, but we often react based on the past. May the true creative liberty of the Holy Spirit be set free in our churches to demonstrate the glorious variety of our God!

Kelly Willard

Kelly Willard started in music ministry at the tender age of 13. It was then that she regularly visited nursing homes and participated in Sunday and weekday services at her home church in Winter Haven, Florida. She also began writing songs at that time. In the years to follow, she found herself playing piano and singing in various gospel and contemporary Christian music groups, such as "The Archers," "Harlan Rogers & Friends" and others.

It was not until she was 22 years old and had been married for four years that her first solo recording, entitled "Blame it on the One I Love," was made and released by Maranatha! Music.

Kelly has subsequently done several other solo projects. All along the way Kelly has enjoyed what she considers "giving my gifts freely back to the Lord by supporting my fellow Christian artists," as she has gladly participated when asked to sing duets or background vocals. She has joined such artists as Twila Paris, Paul Overstreet, Ricky Skaggs, Buddy Green, and many others in that capacity. Additionally she has sung on many Maranatha! Music Praise recordings and Integrity's Hosanna! Music Praise projects.

Kelly attends Belmont Church in Nashville, Tennessee, and frequently assists in worship leading there. Kelly and her husband, Dan, live in the Nashville area and have two children, Bryan and Haylie.

You Can Only Lead Where You Are Going

In my early years of ministry I honestly did not realize that I led people into worshiping God. All I knew was that, out of my own personal need and desperation, I sang my songs directly to the Lord. I never really knew the impact my singing had on people until I began to hear back from them (a few here and there) the stories of the effect my voice and songs were having on their relationship with God. That to me was a great blessing, but it also presented a great challenge for me from that time forth.

The challenge has been for me to be sure that I don't consciously try to "move" people by my singing, lest I enter into emotionally manipulating people, which I consider "spiritual witchcraft." I have discovered that my real role in leading people into the worship of God is to go there myself, just as I had always done before I became aware of the effect my personal worship had on others. To confirm this fact, I remember the Holy Spirit once speaking very specifically to my heart.

We were attending Newport-Mesa Christian Center is Costa Mesa, California several years ago. One particular Sunday evening I was asked to sing. As I was trying to prepare my song list for that night, I distinctly sensed the Lord impressing an instruction upon my heart and mind. He said, "I want you to begin to sing more of the worship choruses that you love to sing so much anyway. You just focus on Me, love and worship Me, and while you are singing I will be doing things in people's hearts that you know not of. This is your part from now on."

This has been my constant endeavor ever since. I am convinced that you cannot take someone with you to a place that you are not going yourself. In order to be *leading* in worship, I must be worshiping the Lord myself.

I have also found that it is not our responsibility as worship leaders, if someone does or does not choose to go with us into the Lord's presence. Our part (as worship leader) is to go before the Lord in sincere love and adoration of Him. Those who witness that and want to come along, will come do so. (This revelation has relieved a major amount of stress from my worship leading!)

Worshiping God and leading His people into His presence is the greatest pleasure and privilege I know.

Curt Coffield

Curt Coffield loves helping others worship. He is the associate pastor of music ministries at Resurrection Life Church in Grandville, Michigan. He and his wife, Jennifer, lead the worship for this congregation of over 4000 worshipers in the Grand Rapids area. Curt uses a variety of styles and songs in an effort to serve the congregation and give each person a chance to "own" their worship experience.

Curt began leading worship in high school. He later attended Christ for the Nations Institute (CFNI) and traveled with Living Praise where he met Jennifer. Curt credits CFNI with imparting to him a burning heart for worship and missions. After college, Curt was the music director for Christian Outreach International where he directed music teams on outreaches throughout eastern Europe and South America. In 1995 he came to Resurrection Life Church. He continues to take teams on overseas outreaches every year.

In the past few years, Curt and Jennifer have had the privilege of leading the music team at their church in two recording projects, "Blessed to be a Blessing" and "House of Praise." Curt is also a song writer and has songs recorded by CFNI and featured in Worship Leader *magazine's "Song Discovery."*

Curt and Jennifer have been married for seven years and reside in Grandville.

The Toilet Paper Tale—
And Other Humble Happenings

I'm sure you know the feeling. It comes in like a flood. The progression can go something like this:

"Oh, wow, people are laughing. Something *must* be funny. I wonder what's *so* funny. Are they laughing at *me*? What about *me* could be that funny?"

Then comes... "the moment." It's the moment you discover what *is* so funny about yourself. I've known this feeling too many times to number...

One particular evening we were having a guest speaker. The church was packed with upwards of 2000 people and the worship had been extra exciting. Following the worship, I left the platform, briefly visited the restroom and then proceeded to find my seat next to my wife near the front.

It started with a snicker, but quickly gained momentum. As I walked down the aisle, the laughter claimed me as its subject. It was not until I reached the front of the auditorium that I successfully completed my investigation as to the reason for the outbreak. I glanced down and discovered that a piece of toilet paper had married itself to the heel of my shoe and followed me into the service. It had been sailing in the wind like the tail of a kite, coming in at a whopping 30 inches long! And oh, was it comical!

It so shocked me that I instantly shook it from my shoe as I would shake off a snake going in for the kill. My wife Jennifer's eyes reflected my horror as I sat down next to her. I rattled off what had just happened and she, fighting off the urge to join the laughter, asked the obvious, "Where is it now?" There it sat in the aisle, a memorial to the humility it had just so matter-of-factly handed out. I later learned that a faithful usher had humbly come to my rescue and discretely removed the troublemaker from the service.

So what's the point? The point is: *embarrassing things happen to worship leaders*. These embarrassing things have a purpose in our lives. Would you believe that eventually it's possible to become immune to embarrassment? I don't want to get into the deeply challenging theological debate over whether or not God sends embarrassment. I just know that out of these situations God can cause humility to grow in us. Humility is vital to being effective in our effort to lead others into being honest and real in their adoration of our Lord.

The truth is that as worship leaders we are continually in the place where mistakes, goofs, and mishaps occur. Accept that! Don't allow the American mentality of "perfectionism" to have its way. We must put aside the self-consciousness that keeps us from the ability to keep others focused on the Holy Spirit even when we blunder. We have to come to the place were we allow others to see our weaknesses without being ashamed.

So you forget the lyrics...or start the wrong song... or break a string...or mischord...or start the song too fast or too slow. Is the focus now on you as you attempt to deal with the damage done to your ego, or do you allow God to bring you to the place where those things no longer undermine your confidence?

Please don't misunderstand the point. I'm not encouraging you to ignore these situations or to act as if they're not happening. I'm not asking you to dismiss the need for excellence. I'm not even telling you to "get through." I'm begging you to take a step back, embrace the reality of worship, and realize how unimportant our "image" is in this thing. People need someone "real" to lead them in their worship.

Don't fall into the trap of our day: an obsession with image and perfection. We frequently elect government officials on image. We buy music, often not for the artistry of the music, but for the image of the artist. Allow your image to become less and less important. Our desire is to see people worship God because He is God, not because of a certain persona that we can simulate.

Resist thoughts like: "Oh no, people must think I'm a geek," and embrace the Lord. Our prayer should be,

"God, I'm willing to be whoever I need to be and look however I need to look, if it makes You more real and reachable in worship."

I'd like to be able to say that I have totally mastered this discipline, but I can't. This willingness to place ourselves in vulnerable positions in serving our congregation can go beyond the borders of worship. About two years ago the director of Women's Ministry at our church asked my wife and me to sing for the "Ladies' Spring Tea." With reservations, I reluctantly agreed. As the event grew closer, the reality began to set in that I would be the only "guy" in this group of 400 women.

Things got worse! We were asked to sing: "Don't Sit Under the Apple Tree with Anyone Else But Me," a song from the '30s! My mind began to work: "What will people think? I'm a worship leader. I never signed up for *this*! This is *not* me." Have you ever caught yourself with such thoughts?

The evening came. I tried to disguise my negative attitude as best as possible. Jen and I sang, and then I jetted from the building eager to reclaim my masculinity. Thank God for His grace that redeems us from such self-centeredness. The next week I was walking through the church, and Mary, a beautiful grandmother and saint of the faith took me aside to share what the experience had meant to her. Mary is one of the most encouraging people in all of the church. She's always there in services with her hands raised to God, pouring her heart out to

Him in worship. No matter how new and contemporary the chorus, she never misses a beat.

Well, here I stood following the "Tea," with Mary, teary-eyed, sharing how special the song "Don't Sit Under the Apple Tree" was to her. She explained that it was her husband's and her favorite song when they were dating, and it had been years since she had heard it. She had appreciated hearing Jen and I sing it, as it had brought back such special memories.

There I stood—*stunned*. Do the words "subtle Holy Spirit rebuke" mean anything to you? To think that such ministry could occur in such a vulnerable, seemingly embarrassing place! God broke something in me standing right there in the hall. I literally fled to my office and cried before God, asking Him to remove the pride of my heart. I truly believe that through this incident, God "grew" me in my effectiveness as a worship leader, helping me to become more immune to this sense of embarrassment.

I recall the time that Jen and I were leading in the Worship band at CFNI. We had been out of school for 6 years and were so honored to be asked to come and lead worship for the student body. As we were worshiping, my guitar chose to release these "yells from hell." I fought the temptation to think, "These kids must think, 'What an idiot, get a real guitar.'" Instead I tried, in God's grace, not to become crippled with embarrassment and thus be rendered ineffective. I simply continued to worship God. Later I realized that it was actually beneficial for those students to see that times of worship don't always go perfectly, and that in those moments we can still continue to stay focused on God and our desire for more of Him.

Then there was the time we were opening a service with David Baroni's song "Ain't Gonna Let No Rock." What a great song! We had always started the song with a slow verse first. I got the bright idea to start it in the middle of the chorus, a capella (trust me, don't try it). Walking out on the platform, Karen, our choir director asked, "Where will we get the pitch for our first note?" I confidently said, "Oh, I'll strum out the chord and we'll get it." I sang out the first note with the choir and ensemble joining in hopeful confidence, but by the second chord, it was obvious we were miles away from the real key. I pulled the whole thing to a stop and started again... with the same result. It was another opportunity to become crippled with embarrassment. Instead, it became a moment of being real and not overly "slick." I took a moment to allow everyone to laugh about the obvious. I shared my heart for a moment, being real and not over-spiritualizing the situation. It was a true moment of bonding with our congregation. We eventually started the song; and I'll guarantee no rocks cried out for us that night. An experience that could have sent at least those on the platform home for the evening instead displayed our "realness" and made the platform feel less like a "stage."

Be willing to laugh at yourself. Be willing to be real. Take on no sense of image or mystique. Take on Christ and His willingness to become but a servant that others may know God. By the way, on the night of the adorning toilet paper incident, I returned to the platform at the end of the night to lead those who had been laughing into worship. I can honestly say I was not hindered by the incident. Instead, I added to the numerous other stories of how God causes us to grow in our service to others in order to serve Him.

Scott Wesley Brown

Scott Wesley Brown has left an indelible mark on Christian music. The past two decades have seen his signature on no fewer than nine number-one singles in Adult-Contemporary and Christian music rankings. His songs have been recorded by Sandi Patti, Amy Grant, Bruce Carroll, Pat Boone, The Imperials, Petra and international opera star Placido Domingo.

Integrity's Hosanna! Music release "Mission of Praise" is Scott's 18th album and really captures his heart for world evangelization. His newest release, "More Like You" (Threefold Music) is an exciting collection of new worship songs. He is also a featured singer at Promise Keepers events and has written several songs for them including the number-one radio single, "Godly Men."

A real highlight for Scott was his participation in the first publicly promoted Christian music event in the U.S.S.R. It was during this August, 1989 concert that over 15,000 Soviets heard the passionate cry for love and compassion while the Spirit moved some 2000 to join the family of Christ. Scott has taken more than 100 musicians on trips to the mission field and provided hundreds of musical instruments to musicians and missionaries in Third World and restricted-access countries.

Scott, his wife, Belinda, and their two daughters, Jessica and Hannah, live in Franklin, Tennessee.

Skip Chose John

When I was in college I served as a volunteer leader for a high school ministry called Young Life. Once a week we would hold a "club" meeting in the home of one of the high school kids who was involved with the program. There were three people who led the club: Skip, John, and myself. Skip was the Area Director for Young Life. He had started the ministry in this particular high school and had kept it going ever since. He was a brilliant theologian and speaker with a seminary education. His stirring gospel messages at the end of each club meeting made me want to accept Christ all over again.

John was a local college student who was quiet, yet friendly. He didn't have much talent in the speaking or singing department. He basically just hung around with the kids. On the other hand, I was given charge over the song leading and cherished every moment of it. I could razzle and dazzle the kids with my guitar riffs. I felt confident whenever I spoke in front of the club and could be really funny in the crazy skits we performed each night.

John seemed to stumble through his words, and he wasn't very funny in the skits.

Young Life was the ultimate for me, and I was convinced that when our leader Skip left to start a new club in another high school, he would leave me in charge of the existing club.

The reasons were all apparent. I could lead singing. I added lots of life to the skits. I could give a good gospel message and invitation. I was the obvious choice. But when Skip made his final decision, he chose John. I had to gasp for air. I couldn't believe it. When I asked Skip for a reason, what he told me has echoed in my heart time and time again.

"John wants to want to love Jesus," was Skip's response. I looked stunned. He repeated it again, "John wants to want to love Jesus." Then he said, "Chew on it, Scott." Well, I've been chewing on it ever since.

What does it mean to want to want to love Jesus? What was it in my friend John, that Skip chose over my ability and talent? I think that the main issue was and still is a heart for God rather than simply talent alone. Perhaps that is why, after God called Bezalel as a craftsman for the Tent of Meeting, his first attribute listed is that he was "filled...with the Spirit of God" (Exodus 31:3). I believe this is foundational to all else. It comes before talent and ability. It doesn't negate talent and ability, but prioritizes the "effectual calling" where there is relationship with God over the "vocational calling" where there is service to

God. Bezalel, an artist, is the first person in the Bible described as being filled with God's Spirit. This is what distinguished him from other talented artists and craftsmen of his day.

In Exodus 33, Moses didn't want to proceed into the Promised Land unless God's presence went with Israel. "Then Moses said to Him, 'If Your Presence does not go with us, do not send us up from here. How will anyone know that You are pleased with me and with Your people unless You go with us? What else will distinguish me and Your people from all the other people on the face of the earth?'" (Exodus 33:15-16).

Being in God's presence is what distinguishes Christian musicians from all the other musicians on the face of this earth. That's what makes the difference in us. No amount of strength, talent or human charisma can replace the impact of God's presence. If He is not at work in our lives we will never be able to operate in the full capacity of God's power.

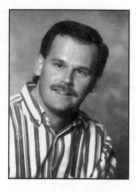

Terry Butler

Terry Butler is a graduate of Azusa Pacific University and has been involved in worship ministry for over 20 years. He is currently an associate pastor at the Pomona/Claremont Vineyard Christian Fellowship in Pomona, California.

Actively involved in training, encouraging and motivating others in worship ministry, Terry participates in many of the Vineyard worship conferences here in the states and abroad. His heart and passion is to see the whole Body of Christ in unity, lifting up and giving glory to the only deserving One.

Among the various worship recordings he has led are "Throne of Grace," "Glory and Honor" and "Before You Now." He has written and co-written numerous worship songs including "Cry of My Heart," "At the Cross" and "The Lord Almighty Reigns."

Terry and his wife have two children and live in Southern California.

Terry Butler

The Evangelistic Power of Worship

———⟨⟩———

It seemed like a typical Sunday morning. Prior to the service there were no powerful revelations from the Lord about what would take place. It seemed like an ordinary day. I was preparing to lead worship.

As I stepped onto the platform I noticed that one of our regular attenders had brought her husband to church for the very first time. She had been praying for him for months. He desperately needed the Lord Jesus in his life but seemed to be a long way from admitting it. His wife had gently invited him to church from time to time but he had resisted. Now, here he was, seated in the congregation.

When the praise and worship began I couldn't help noticing that this man—we'll call him Al—seemed to be really enjoying the music. It wasn't the usual disinterested unsaved heathen scenario. I could tell that he was really trying to follow along and participate. He seemed genuinely interested in what was happening.

As the service progressed the Spirit of God seemed to be moving among us in a gentle way. When we got to the fourth or fifth song I looked over toward Al and noticed that he was weeping. Then something happened I'll never forget.

As we neared the end of the song we were singing, Al stepped out from where he was standing and started down the aisle toward the front of the sanctuary. When he got to

171

the front he knelt down. By this time he was crying very hard and the senior pastor (my father) noticed him and moved to the front to meet him. Meanwhile, the rest of the congregation kept on singing with even more intensity. There were many who realized that God was at work in Al at that very moment. His wife and others close to her were crying tears of joy. There was no doubt that we were witnessing the miracle-working power of God!

At the end of the service we found out that Al had not been in a church service since he was a child. He told us that he felt the Lord powerfully touch him when we began to worship. He said that he couldn't wait to give his heart to God. He had to go to the front to kneel, repent and pray.

As he shared with us, Al indicated that he hoped he hadn't interrupted the service. He was apparently concerned that he might have caused a scene. We told him not to worry; we like those kinds of interruptions!

Al began attending regularly with his wife and grew in the faith. That Sunday, worship evangelism had taken place right before our eyes before the altar call had ever been given. As we lifted our voices and our hearts in praise and adoration to the King, He drew a wayward child to His side.

Don't ever discount what God will do in *your* services as your people turn to Him in worship. He is no respecter of persons. If the Lord did it once, He can do it again. Jesus told us that where two or three gather in His Name that He will be there. Let's expect Him to move in powerful ways as we worship Him.

Chéri Walters

Chéri Walters is minister of creative arts at Canyon Country Assembly of God, in the northernmost part of Los Angeles County. A graduate of Oral Roberts University with a degree in church music, Chéri has directed adult and children's choirs for 23 years in Oklahoma, Florida, and her native California. Together with her husband, Ken, she has served on staff at three churches. They have served their present church, (Ken as senior pastor) for over 12 years, where has Chéri found herself forced to grow into the role of pianist and worship leader.

She is the author of "Advice to the Minister of Music: Get A Giant Hat Rack!" plus over 75 articles published in Worship Leader, Christianity Today, Moody Monthly, Creator Music Magazine, and many others. Chéri is a licensed minister with the Assemblies of God and has served on that denomination's National Music Committee. Chéri juggles church responsibilities with writing, speaking at ministry conferences across the U.S., and being "her kids' mom" to four teens.

Thank God for Botts Dots

Thank God for Botts Dots! You know, those raised reflectors they use to mark the lanes on the highway? There's no telling how many lives have been saved by those little bumps in the road.

I recall one particular trip when my husband, Ken, his brother, Ron, and I crossed three states and a panhandle in nearly 30 hours, stopping only for gas and pit stops. Exhausted, nearly hypnotized by endless stretches of black pavement outlined with white, we were trying desperately to stay awake. Just 30 more minutes and we'd be at Ken's mom's home. Surely we could make it just 30 more min.... Brrummp.

Startled, Ken jerked the car back into the lane. "You've got to talk to me! Help me stay awake," he said, rubbing his face. "I'm trying," I said, blinking my eyes. Ron snored on in the back seat. Only a few miles from home, we were "driving by Braille"—glazing over at the wheel, drifting out of the lane, only to be roused by the rumble and jolt of the wheels going over the Botts Dots.

After the longest half hour of our lives, we slipped into my mother-in-law's house in the wee hours and crashed (our bodies, not the car) on her couch. Without those little bumps that outline the lanes jolting us, I'm not sure we would have made it. We should have pulled over, taken a nap, something. We know it now; we knew it then. We put ourselves and others on the road in danger in our need to push on.

About two years ago, I went through a season in my life where I felt creatively exhausted and spiritually drained. We'd been at our current church over 10 years, and I just couldn't think of one more variation on the Living Last Supper, or the Christmas musical, or anything else. Leading Sunday morning worship I felt as dry and empty as a husk. Added to that, my oldest was leaving the nest, and it hit me like a ton of bricks: Have I done everything I could and should as a parent? Did I leave anything out? I'd always loved ministry life; now I was beginning to resent it.

I would like to have taken a sabbatical from my responsibilities planning our church's worship services and music/drama outreach productions, but it wasn't possible. So I pushed on. Thank God, He put bumps in the road to warn me and keep me on track.

There was my husband, (who is also my senior pastor), who said, "You don't have to do the Easter production this year," and would even have let me out of Christmas (for which I will always love him)! Whenever I was tempted to rescue other floundering ministries at the church (the women's group needs a leader!) he stopped me. He gave me as much breathing room as he could, and prevented me from driving myself right off the road.

There was my fellow pastor's wife, Candy, who said, "I'm worried about you. What's going on?" She wouldn't take, "Fine" for an answer. Thank God for a good friend who listened to more than just my words, who let me vent without calling me a whiner, and who prayed for me with the spirit and with understanding. Together we agonized over a talented, committed ministry friend who'd pushed herself beyond the limits. This get-the-job-done woman, also a worship leader (among her many other duties), found herself in a grocery store aisle one day, turning around and around, unable to make a decision. Candy and I looked at each other and said, "There, but for the grace of God, go we." We held each other accountable for taking time off, and for letting go of some of our ministry responsibilities (or at least for not taking on any more). Candy's empathy and wise counsel were more bumps, waking me up to the danger, keeping me inside the lines.

There were God's people in our church family who spoke words of encouragement and appreciation at just the right moment. There was my fellow keyboardist, who willingly shared worship-leading responsibilities when first one, then another worship leader moved away. There was Carol, who grew into the role of assistant producer of our Christmas production, relieving me of a thousand-and-one details (along with the accompanying nightmares and cold sweats). There was my mom, a church musician herself, who provided several one or two-day sabbaticals when an extended one was out of reach.

There were retreats and conferences where God refreshed my spirit and rekindled my enthusiasm. There was

God's Spirit, moving through the preaching and reading of His Word, and in the worship times, gently guiding me back into the lane. There were songs like Pam Thum's "Life Is Hard (God Is Good)," that watered my arid inner landscape with my own tears. There were missionaries with videos of hopeless Romanian children that turned me inside out, exposing my selfishness and apathy, reminding me how incredibly blessed I am. These were the Botts Dots that jolted me back to a sense of urgency about ministry, that rumbled and bumped me back between the lines, pointed forward again, this time with joy and purpose.

I would like to have pulled over and rested, but it wasn't possible (at least not without a lot of upheaval to a lot of people). But thank God for the Botts Dots of family and friends, Word and music, partners in ministry, and the little snatches of rest and relaxation we can carve out of busy schedules. Thank God for bumps in the road.

Byron Easterling

Byron Easterling began playing for church services at the age of 10. His first public piano performance was at Powell Symphony Hall in St. Louis at age 12. He attended the University of Miami in Florida where he studied jazz piano and then further studied at Webster College in St. Louis in composition and piano performance. Since that time he has been traveling, speaking and leading worship in churches and conferences from Rome to Los Angeles, Winnipeg to Guatemala —including serving a season with Worship International, Integrity Music's ministry division.

Currently, he is traveling and presenting solo piano concerts utilizing his heart and call for worship evangelism. While on the road, he meets personally with worship pastors, pastors and ministry leaders.

He, his wife, Crystal, and daughter, Kathryn, reside in Fort Worth, Texas, where they are sent out from Shiloh House Community Church.

Be Yourself Before the Lord —Others Will Follow

During the 80s, my wife Crystal and I were on staff with a major Christian organization in their music ministry. We began to present Concerts of Praise after our regular concert season. We were new to worship, and I was ignorant of the status quo for worship leading. I was just plain confused!

We were preparing for 30 worship concerts in the Midwest when it hit me to ask God...what do I do during these concerts of praise? How do I present them?

As I prayed, an obvious reply came, "Worship Me. This is not a performance." Also, a simple system for leading the worship time was laid out for me. In addition I felt impressed to invite the people to confess their sins to God, and if need be, to one another. I wanted to ask the Holy Spirit to come and minister to each person.

At this stage of my life I had no clue what inviting the Spirit of God to minister meant!

So, I did exactly this. I would worship and invite the Holy Spirit to come and minister. I remember night after night looking up and seeing the audience in tears, on their knees, worshiping God, and being touched by God. It was *scary*!! I didn't know what to do. I invite God to come and this is the outcome?

I looked up at Crystal, and with a look of pained desperation, screamed out in silence, "What do I do now?" She looked back and shook her head as if to say, "Hey bud, you started this thing. Don't ask me."

We finished that series of concerts and sat in front of our host's home crying out to the Father, "Please, God, we need to know how to handle what You are doing." The Lord was taking us places we wouldn't have gone if we were not willing to follow His lead. The cry of our hearts is to follow His lead, not a particular system of worship.

When I lead worship I am less concerned about the people than I am worshiping God myself. I have found that if I am honestly connecting with the Lord, the people will follow.

God has placed a style of leading in each worship leader's heart. I am convinced that as you go to your "heart place" in worship—where you simply and honestly worship Him—those around you will enter deeply into His presence with you.

Kim
Bollinger

Kim Bollinger grew up as part of a little country church in Fredericktown, Missouri. Her entire family sang and did much of the music for Sunday services. Her mother played the organ/piano, and her dad, younger brother and sister, and Kim did everything from gospel quartets to trumpet duets! Although Kim remembers loving the Lord from her earliest years, at about 10 years old she made a public confession and was baptized in a local river.

A prolific song writer, Kim's songs have been played and sung around the world. Among her most well-known credits are "Spirit, Touch Your Church" and "I Love to Love You, Lord" both published by Integrity's Hosanna! Music. She has two recordings of her own and is currently prayerfully considering a third. Kim has ministered extensively throughout the United States and overseas. Some of her fondest memories of ministry are from Far Eastern countries.

Presently Kim is the Music Director at Bethesda Evangelical Church in St. Louis, Missouri. She resides in St. Louis with her husband, Scott, and their three daughters.

Beyond My Comfort Zone

⟨≈≋≋≋≋⟩

When I first took the job as music director at a very traditional United Church of Christ, the whole idea seemed out of character for me. My family and I had spent the last 15 years in a non-denominational, "charismatic" environment. For most of those years I sang, played the piano, led worship, or all of the above, with a worship team. The church had a strong focus on worship and prayer. Since my giftings are primarily in the areas of music, and since I love to worship and pray, I and my young family were at church nearly every time the doors were open. My three daughters felt they had a second home, and my husband endured many nights being super dad while I happily labored away at meeting after meeting.

Though not without its problems, the church was a challenging and even "safe" place for us for most of those years. We had developed very close relationships there. It was home to us. We all learned and grew much during that time. Those years in that church were a necessary and vital part of our family's growing process.

There came a season, however, when life at our very comfortable church home became more and more uncomfortable. It is not easy to explain how my family and I went rather quickly from satisfied to unsettled, but that is exactly what happened.

Yes, there were some things going on within the church that my husband and I did not particularly agree with or endorse. I also had my share of wounds and struggled with a relationship or two over the years. However, we were mature enough to recognize that these were part of human nature and church life. We knew that in all facets of life there are difficult situations. We were also experienced enough to know that the perfect church does not exist. Every church has problems.

It was not church problems or even relational difficulties that were causing us to feel as if we were no longer in the place we needed to be. We battled an almost magnetic pull away from our very familiar surroundings. We loved the people and wanted to remain in that comfortable environment, yet something we could not see or understand continued to tug at our hearts as well. We finally began to obey that small, but firm voice and started visiting other churches around our city.

Because we had been so committed and involved before, we had never taken the time to see for ourselves what other fellowship opportunities were available in our area. Though we saw many good things, nothing seemed to be quite right for us.

Transition only got more difficult as time went by. We felt homeless and idle. In the meantime, some very dear friends of ours, who were also going through a transitional time, ended up moving to another state. How we missed them and others who we saw less of than before.

Many lonely days followed as we walked down an unknown and unfamiliar road.

Many people did not understand what we were doing or why. (The truth is, neither did we!) Some were angry with us. Others, for lack of knowing what to say, said nothing at all. There were a handful of loved ones who continued to check on us and love us through that difficult time. Of all the relationships of our lives, those have been the most endearing!

Though we were blessed with those few special relationships, we still battled hurt, loneliness and rejection. I remember thinking I would never again become so involved in a church body. It just hurt too much to have to deal with all we were going through. I prayed, "Lord, if You ever want me to do this again somewhere else, You will have to write it on the wall for me or bring someone to my front door so it will be very clear!"

Never before had I entered a tunnel of time that was so dark. We could not see the light at the end, only the Light that illuminated each step as we went. We could only trust that the Lord knew what was ahead and that He had us in the shadow of His very large wings.

During that period I learned much about the Lord, my Refuge. Some of my most tender moments were spent in worship in the presence of my Father. How I've come to appreciate His grace in the midst of the whirlwind of life. Though there were hours of extreme loneliness and pain, somehow His love would break through and fill me with overwhelming love that carried me on!

Finally, one day, almost two years later, there was a message on my answering machine asking if I would be interested in interviewing for a music director position at a church about ten minutes from where we live. As I picked up the phone to return the call, my doorbell rang. It was the pastor whose voice I had just heard on the telephone message!

The pastor introduced himself and apologized for just showing up at my front door. He had just come from a local Christian radio station to advertise about the opening and ran into a friend of mine who happened to work there. She suggested—no *insisted*—he get in touch with me about the job. As he was driving home, he felt he should just stop by and meet me.

Although I was surprised and cautious, I couldn't just turn down his offer. We talked for over an hour about the vision of his church and I attempted to describe myself to him. After he left, the Lord reminded me of the prayers I had prayed, particularly the one asking Him to bring someone to my door if He wanted me to get back involved in ministry in a local church. Somehow I knew I was in the center of a plan that I knew nothing about!

The Lord was directing my path and even opening a door for me to walk through. "But," I argued, "what about the rest of the family? Lord, what if they don't like this new place? What if *I* don't like it?" Each time I asked, I got a very gentle response, "Will you follow Me?"

Although I realized I had probably been too comfortable in the past, this seemed very extreme to me! A mainline, traditional church!? I hadn't set foot in one since my childhood! Africa seemed a little less intimidating! I was used to spontaneity and freedom of expression. Was God actually moving me—sanguine, spunky, love-to-worship, Kim—into a staid, bulletin-binding, hymn-hugging denomination?!! What a radical idea. Talk about a challenge.

Well, after much discussion and prayer with my husband, I accepted the position. My mind was rolling its eyes, but my heart knew this was right. The Lord had answered my somewhat sarcastic prayer, and now I needed to get serious about what was ahead. Slowly I found that the Lord was filling me with new vision and strategy to move forward.

Little by little I have begun to accept this new mission. I've found that there are truly wonderful things happening in this warm little church. I've seen a spark turn into a flame first in many in the church and then in me. There is a hunger for renewal and new life in the Lord Jesus.

I've come to realize that being comfortable is not what Christianity is about! Obedience and trust appear to be closer to God's main agenda for us.

There is a great job to be done in the earth today for the sake of the eternal kingdom of God. Being willing to go beyond our comfort zones to serve and bring the gospel message is something for which true worship leaders need to prepare themselves. By His grace let us prepare to obey even when it means setting aside lifestyles and things that are dear to us. Obedience is better than sacrifice (1 Samuel 15:22), but many times obedience requires sacrifice.

I thank the Lord for teaching me more and more about living for Him. May we as worshipers be encouraged not to get comfortable in our victories, but be willing to move on to new ones as almighty God would lead.

Leann Albrecht

Leann Albrecht has been a studio singer and worship leader for the past 15 years. She has worked with artists such as Amy Grant, Michael W. Smith, Don Moen, Ron Kenoly and Alvin Slaughter. Leann appears on over 75 Integrity Music projects as well as Maranatha's Praise Band 7 and 8.

Some of her classic solo work include "I Worship You," "Shout to the Lord" and "Lead Me to the Rock" as well as many others on Integrity recordings.

Leann is currently leading worship for the Women of Faith "Bring Back the Joy" conferences as well as partnering with Kim Hill for Focus on the Family's "Renewing the Heart" conferences. She is also a leader and clinician for Maranatha's Praise Band Worship Leader Workshop conferences.

"Verses for the King" is her brand new solo album project just released in January.

Leann currently resides in Nashville, Tennessee, with her husband, Carl.

Right Where You Are

Quite some time ago I was asked to be a part of a worship team for a special service at our church. I knew the guest speaker would probably want more singing and more personal ministry and prayer time than we normally had.

When the actual night of the service arrived I felt very empty and needy. Honestly, church was the last place on earth I wanted to be. I was certain that I had nothing to give, nothing to offer to anyone that would benefit them. What was I doing up front "ministering"? The "sacrifice of praise" was far from reality to me. I was there purely out of commitment, certainly not desire.

The service began, and we led the congregation in praise and worship. Then as the guest speaker began to minister and pray for people, God moved powerfully. People were healed and set free in obviously miraculous ways. It was awesome to see!

However, as these things began to happen I became increasingly frustrated because I was bound to the microphone. All I wanted to do was get off the platform and into the nearest prayer line, but I was obligated to continue singing as part of the worship team. As the service continued on at length, it seemed as though there would never be an opportunity for the personal ministry I felt I needed.

I began to complain to the Lord about my dilemma.

He quickly responded with a rebuke. In essence He said, "I am not a respecter of persons. I am everywhere at all times. Do you not believe that I can minister to you right here where you are without the laying on of anyone's hands?"

Immediately, I was convicted of my short sightedness. I had been guilty of not fully recognizing the bigness of God. Lynn DeShazo expressed it well in her song *Be Magnified*, when she said, "I have made You too small in my eyes, O Lord, forgive me."

I asked God to forgive me and released my neediness to Him. I then redirected my focus to Him. As I did so, I was suddenly overwhelmed with the weightiness of His presence. The next thing I knew, I was trying to pick myself up off the floor. I had collapsed under the power of the Lord. No one had touched me or laid hands on me in prayer, only the invisible presence of the Holy Spirit. I had never experienced anything like that before.

I began to weep as I thought of His unwavering faithfulness to meet me wherever I was, in whatever state, whatever the need! His love for me covered all of that.

Since then I have become a worship leader. This experience always reminds me that no matter how inadequate or unprepared I feel, the grace and faithfulness of the Lord will meet me wherever I am. I know that He will make up for all that I am lacking. The key responsibility I have is to keep my eyes fixed on His greatness instead of my weakness. I cling to 2 Corinthians 12:9 "...for my power is made perfect in weakness."

Tommy Coomes

Tommy Coomes was a pioneer of contemporary Christian music in the 70s as a member of the band Love Song and was a record producer and the Creative Director at Maranatha! Music in the 70s, 80s and 90s. He produced or executive produced several hundred recordings, including the popular Praise Series.

Tommy loves to innovate, create and influence the church to worship and witness. He founded The Praise Band in 1989 to explore new forms of worship and evangelism and has ministered around the world with Franklin Graham, Billy Graham, and Greg Laurie's Harvest Crusades.

Tommy pioneered the Maranatha Music Worship Leaders Workshops in 1991 to train and equip the church in contemporary forms of worship. In 1992 he formed and led the Maranatha! Promise Band to serve the growing Promise Keepers movement.

As a speaker, teacher and consultant, Tommy's background draws on a depth of experience as a singer, song writer, producer, performer and worship leader. His greatest joy is "to know Him and make Him known."

Tommy and his wife, Shelley, live in Southern California with their two sons, Tyler and Erick—both musicians.

His ministry statement is reflected in Psalm 40:3: "He has put a new song in my mouth, a hymn of praise to our God. Many will see and fear and put their trust in the Lord."

Looking Past the Differences

During the early 1970's I was privileged to be a part of Love Song, one of the very first contemporary Christian music bands. The members of this group were tremendous musicians and singers. Some had previously opened for groups like Three Dog Night and Grateful Dead and had had several hit records. We were all in our early twenties. We all had one other thing in common: very little experience with church.

We found Christ in a small, informal church called Calvary Chapel in Costa Mesa, California. Pastor Chuck Smith, Sr., and his wife Kay had a tremendous heart for young people. Many kids in their teens and twenties were coming to the Lord and being baptized in the Pacific Ocean. The media called it "The Jesus Movement."

Love Song was a contemporary Christian group, but worship was always a big part of our ministry. I wrote the first worship song recorded by Maranatha! Music and produced the Praise Album Series. Chuck Girard, another member of the Love Song, has written many great worship songs and continues to sing and teach around the world. Helping others find Christ and worship Him was what we were all about. It's still what we are about!

Psalm 40:3 declares: "He has put a new song in my mouth, a song of praise. Many shall see and fear and put their trust in the Lord." That was our experience. God changed our lives. His Spirit put a new song in our hearts. But this "new song" was also in a new form that many "churched" people had to stop and think about. Was it genuine? Was it sacred? Was it secular?

We experienced a variety of responses to our "new song." Many were saved. Many wrote us off. Some would weep while others found new joy. Some were confused and fearful. New things are often messy. We were young and naive and had some lessons to learn about God and about His people. One of the greatest lessons we learned came out of one of our greatest personal rejections.

We were only a few months old in the Lord when a Bible teacher informally invited us to sing at a Full Gospel Businessmen's Convention in Oakland, California. I'm not sure what we expected to find at the end of our 500 mile drive, but we were shocked. It was suits and ties, chiffon dresses and hair spray as far as the eye could see. (Remember, this was the early 70s!) We, on the other hand, looked more like where we had been than where we were going.

When we walked into this formal setting, it reminded me of the parting of the Red Sea. We were so out of place that everyone immediately started moving away from us as fast as they could go. It was apparent that these people did not want us in their "nice" convention. They were rude to us. Unfortunately, we were quick to privately criticize their actions. We had not experienced anything like this in Southern California. The older, more conservative Christians there had welcomed us and were happy that our lives were changing.

It should be understood that every kind of radical, political and anti-establishment faction imaginable was alive and well in this, the Bay area, during the late 60s and early 70s. What we didn't know was that one of these militant groups had disrupted this same meeting the year before.

The head of the convention—we nicknamed him "Cool Hand Luke"—was afraid that we represented a new disruption and made it very clear to us that this was *his* convention and that he had no intention of letting us sing. It didn't matter who knew us or who had invited us!

After two long days of rejection and growing disdain, we found ourselves at a Sunday morning prayer breakfast. An impromptu meeting was being held by the leaders and speakers at their long table at the front of the ballroom.

It was funny. It looked like a football team in a huddle. Every once in a while someone would peek out and point back to the corner where we were and then go right back into the huddle. The speaker who had invited us was asking Demos Shakarian for his permission to let us sing that morning. A messenger appeared from the huddle and walked toward us. "Why don't you get your guitars and be ready to sing one song," he said.

As we approached the platform, Cool Hand Luke was there to greet us. He was not happy that someone had gone over his head. He grabbed my arm so hard that I thought he would break it. He looked me in the eye, gritted his teeth and said, "One song and no talking." I was shaking like a leaf! I was just a few months old in the Lord and didn't understand the politics and power struggles that were going on. I just wanted to sing for Jesus.

We filed onto the stage with two acoustic guitars and a violin and formed a semi-circle around the lone microphone. I'm sure the people in the audience were wondering, "Who let these guys in here? How did they get on the stage?" We sang one song—"Welcome Back."

As we began to sing, something happened that I've never seen before or since. As I looked out over the large room full of people, it appeared as though a wave was rolling from the right side of the room to the left. I live in California near the ocean where I'm used to watching the waves roll in. This was a wave of the Holy Spirit. People began to weep as He touched them.

It was as though eyes were suddenly opened. We were all able to look past the outward appearance. The Bible says, "Man looks at the outward appearance, but the LORD looks at the heart" (1 Samuel 16:7). People saw God at work in a way that they didn't expect. Suddenly everything changed.

Cool Hand Luke quickly appeared and asked us to share our testimonies, one at a time. It took twenty minutes. Then he asked us sing a second song.

Bob Mumford was the guest speaker that day. He gave us a great lesson on God's secret weapon: Agape love. When people don't love you, just pull out your secret weapon and love them anyway.

After the service was over I witnessed one of the most amazing demonstrations of the miracle-working power of God's love I have ever seen. A five-foot tall white lady with silver hair approached a very tall black man with a huge Afro. As she reached up to hug this six-and-a-half-foot ex-Black Panther, who was now a new Christian, she looked straight into his eyes and said, "You know, before today I could never love anybody that looked like you." Tears filled their eyes and mine.

God removed the veil from all of our eyes that day. We learned that His love is able to do things that we can not do on our own. We began to understand that His love is what binds us together. It's His love and Spirit that we must look for. Our job is to serve Him. People are afraid of change. We should expect that, but at the same time, we must pray for God to build a bridge by His Spirit. We have seen Him answer that prayer over and over again.

There may be people in your church who look differently or act differently than you. You might not like them. They might not like you or your music. However, God has called us to love. That love goes beyond all outward differences.

I'll never forget the lesson we learned that day in Oakland. It has guided me every day of my ministry. I still have the audio tape of that morning's service. The label says, "Testimony of Converted Hippies"! It also says, "God's Secret Weapon."

Rob Packer

Rob Packer has been involved in Christian music for the last 30 years. Beginning in 1980, he was music director at Parklands Baptist Church in Christchurch, New Zealand, for three years. From there he went on to North Shore Faith Centre in Auckland for seven years. During this time in Auckland Rob pioneered the National Worship Ministry Conferences from 1986 through 1988 and developed a system for distributing new worship songs throughout the churches in New Zealand.

Rob is a song writer, having written songs such as "Victor's Crown," "No Other Name," and "Fan the Flame." He has taught worship seminars in New Zealand, Australia, Tonga, Singapore, Malaysia, Scotland and the U.S.A. He is involved in Lifeway Ministries, a Christian training college, where he is involved in worship ministry, lecturing, and pastoral ministry at Beachland Christian Centre, a local church based at Lifeway Ministries.

Rob, his wife, Lyn, and their children, Daniel and Tanya, live in Snells Beach, a small town an hour north of Auckland, New Zealand.

We Must Listen to Hear God's Voice

During the early stages of my involvement in the ministry of worship, I was part of a church that had relatively shorter times of worship and little congregational expression of "free praise" or spontaneous worship. From that beginning, the Lord led me to a church in another city that placed a major emphasis on the worship aspect of the service. The people in this church were accustomed to worshiping for about an hour at a time, and a large part of that time would involve free praise and congregational response to the Holy Spirit. This was very different from that with which I was familiar.

On the first Sunday I was to minister in this new church I was asked to play the piano and help lead the people in the time of worship. I felt as though I had just been thrown into the deep end and it was a sink or swim situation! I was constantly looking at the worship pastor and hoping for facial or verbal signals that would give me some idea as to where to go next. I felt quite lost in the whole situation.

As time went by people in the church described to me experiences that they had had in worship. I could only try to imagine what it would have been like. I had no previous experience like theirs that could give me any idea as to what to aim for in a worship time or how to lead the people there. There was no spoken pressure put on me, and yet I did feel a real pressure to "come up with the goods" and lead the people into the presence of God. Those were frustrating days!

During that time the cry of my heart was, "Lord, please make me sensitive to the moving of the Holy Spirit in the meetings!" Unfortunately, because there was no apparent immediate answer, it seemed to me that God was being mean and stingy! He didn't pour out a large measure of sensitivity on me or even change me in any way at all at that point in time. However, over the next few months I sensed Him telling me, "Rob, your sensitivity to Me during the course of a corporate time of worship will be in exact proportion to your sensitivity to My voice during the week."

That was not the answer I was looking for. In fact, it was an extremely frustrating answer because I wanted an immediate solution. However, it forced me to look at a far more important issue: my entire relationship with Him. Was there a continual awareness of His presence with me? Did I have a heart that was waiting for—and listening to—His quiet prompting? Was I responding in obedience to what I sensed? Was I including Him in the conversations that would go around in my mind in the course of a day?

I found that it was as simple as asking Him, "Father, I really need to know what to say to help this person I'm speaking to." Or, "Lord, I need a new pair of shoes, and I want to be a good steward of Your money, so please help me find the best deal."

As I listened more to the thoughts that God would put in my mind, and not dismiss them as being "just me," I found that He was speaking a lot more frequently than I had originally thought.

I began to practice the lost art of *listening*. In doing this, over the months and years I found that when it came to preparing for a time of corporate worship it was much easier to hear His voice. I had a greater confidence to follow in obedience what I was sensing.

As I look back on my journey with the Lord, I would say that the process of developing sensitivity to His voice has been slower that I would have liked. However, I have grown much in this regard through the years and I continue to grow. I have no intention of stopping or slowing down. The rewards are too wonderful for that!

Andy Park

Andy Park was born and raised in the San Fernando Valley, a suburb of Los Angeles. At 17, Andy came to a deeper relationship with Jesus Christ. Upon entering UCLA, he became involved in Bible studies and fellowship groups.

At the Vineyard Christian Fellowship in Reseda, California, he began his involvement in worship leading and song writing. Andy wrote and performed a variety of styles of contemporary Christian music. Through the early 1980s his focus began to shift more to writing worship songs. He moved to Langley, British Columbia, and joined the Langley Vineyard church plant, where he was on staff for four years as an assistant pastor.

In the 1980s Andy led worship for John Wimber conferences domestically and internationally and first recorded with Vineyard Music Group. He has since led worship on several "Touching The Father's Heart" series recordings, recorded an acoustic worship album and has contributed to several of the "Winds Of Worship" albums. Andy's songs include "The River is Here" and "Spirit of the Sovereign Lord."

Andy and his wife, Linda, are the parents of six beautiful children: Zachary, David, Michael, Jessica, Benjamin, and Isaac.

Fulfill Your Calling,
Not Someone Else's

In my early 20s I served as an intern pastor in two different churches where the pastors were very gifted. Both of them were skilled teachers and had the ability to draw large numbers of people through their teaching and charismatic personalities. At that point in my life I wasn't sure what I was supposed to do with my life. I thought maybe I was headed for full-time ministry, but when I compared myself with these gifted leaders I couldn't see how I would "make the grade" in the ministry. I definitely was uncertain how the particular mix of spiritual gifts God had given me would enable me to excel in pastoral work.

In those years I led small groups, taught Bible studies, counseled younger Christians, and led worship. I did reasonably well in these areas of ministry, but I wasn't setting the world on fire as an evangelist or drawing great numbers to the groups that I led. My greatest strength was always in the musical area, and I had lesser gifts in the other areas. I wanted to be faithful to use my gifts to their fullest potential to serve God, but I just didn't see how I could possibly fit into a church staff position. I also wondered if my quiet personality would be a liability in becoming a successful pastor.

In the midst of this time of struggling and soul searching, I was invited to join a church planting team in Langley, British Columbia. My wife, Linda, and I had met Gary and Joy Best the previous summer on a ministry trip and had struck up a warm relationship with them. After checking out the area where Gary and Joy were planting the church and getting to know the leadership team, we decided it was the right thing to do.

In my staff position at Langley I majored in worship while working in various other areas of ministry. All of a sudden I found myself in an environment in which I thrived. I was encouraged to develop worship leaders for small groups and Sunday services. I enjoyed doing this. I met with some success, and I've been doing it ever since. I was amazed at the turnaround I had seen in my ministry in such a short period of time. Even though I wasn't a dynamic speaker with a magnetic personality, God could use me to impart the heart and skills required to be a worship leader.

This was the first of many experiences I've had to learn not to compare myself with other ministers. I was measuring my worth and calling as a minister against the gifts and callings that He had given to others. I began to see that all I had to do was minister in the gifts and strength God had given me. Take it from the apostle Peter: "Each one should use whatever gift he has received to serve others, faithfully administering God's grace in its various forms. If anyone speaks, he should do it as one speaking the very words of God. If anyone serves, he should do it with the strength God provides, so that in all things God may be praised through Jesus Christ. To Him be the glory and the power for ever and ever. Amen" (1 Peter 4:10-11).

This Scripture contains essential lessons for the worship leader. First, we all have different gifts. Although we can sharpen the tools God gives us, we can't determine what those tools are. Our tendency is to see a greatly gifted person and ask "Why couldn't I have been given that ability?" Over and over again I marvel at the sovereignty of God—the way He calls and endows each person uniquely. Many times I've had to repent from jealousy of another's gift or position and realize that God is the boss. "There are different kinds of gifts, but the same Spirit. There are different kinds of service but the same Lord. There are different kinds of working but the same God works them in all men" (1 Corinthians 12:4-6). *He* is the only source of our gifts. If we forget that every good gift comes from God, we are liable to stand in awe of the gifted leaders around us instead of giving glory to God.

In this world where success is defined by climbing the ladder so that you can have great power and influence, we must re-educate ourselves according to God's values. According to Peter's exhortation, if we are faithful to give away whatever He has given us, we have found success. Success equals obedience. All I have to do is minister in the strength God provides for me, not the strength He gives to another. When we arrive in heaven and see Jesus, He won't ask us, "How many people did you minister to for Me?" He'll ask, "Were you faithful to use all the talents I gave you for My kingdom?"

My problem of comparing myself to others didn't stop with round one. As I was exposed to more worship leaders, I saw people with great expertise, either vocal or instrumental ability or skill in song writing. In the midst of this I had a hard time not being envious of the things they could do. Confessing my weakness to God and others, I gradually learned to rejoice in the success of others and thank God for raising up other gifted people. God began to plant in me a generous, unselfish heart so that I could be genuinely happy when others around me were reaching new heights in worship leading. I don't think there was any magical moment in this process. It was simply a matter of being relentless to gain the heart of God and turn away from my self-centeredness.

It all cones into clear perspective when we "use whatever gifts we have to serve others, faithfully administering God's grace in its various forms" (1 Peter 4:10). I like to think of it as being a mail carrier. I pick up the packages at the post office and simply deliver them to the people. I can be careful in how I deliver the packages, but I can't really determine what's inside of them. I'm simply giving away whatever I get from God. He determines the size and contents of the gift.

Sally Morgenthaler

Sally Morgenthaler has been active in worship ministry for over 15 years. Her book, Worship Evangelism: Inviting Unbelievers into the Presence of God *(Zondervan, 1995), has become a touchstone for worship-centered ministry and a work whose popularity spans denominational boundaries. She has been a featured speaker at numerous worship conferences including Maranatha! Music's Worship Leader Weekends, Music Minnesota, Net Results: Evangelism Connections, and Leadership Network Forums.*

Sally writes the "Contemporary Worship" column for Worship Leader magazine and is a member of the advisory board to Church Musician Today. Her landmark article, "The Dynamics of Healthy Worship Change," appears in the recently released Celebration Hymnal *(Word) and has been reprinted in several major publications.*

Founder of Worship Evangelism Concepts, Sally is currently helping "twenty-something" congregations develop worship-driven ministry models. She also consults with churches who wish to develop worship services that are substance-faithful yet culturally accessible to the unchurched.

God Calling. For Heaven's Sake, Answer the Phone.

As an almost three-year-old, I was absolutely mesmerized with the aging upright that dominated our family dining room. The old clunker was way past its prime, with dents in its dents and chips in its ivories the size of lima beans. Yet, it was the most fascinating object in my world, a colossal magnet for my miniature hands. I fingered the keys each time I passed. Considering that the piano was situated between the kitchen and the rest of the house, I carried out this mischievous ritual umpteen times a day!

Sometimes, I'd actually stop long enough to play in a more orchestrated fashion. One fall day, my mother was washing the breakfast dishes when she heard me climb onto the narrow bench and plop myself into concert position. From the first smash of the keys, she knew this performance was going to be different. Every motion, every connection was absolutely intense. Staccato blows landed one right after the other, first in the low register, then extending to the uppermost keys and down again. Again and again. My mother, wise woman that she was, figured out at least two things as I punished that poor keyboard: I'd probably had too much brown sugar on my oatmeal, but more importantly, I was inhabiting quite another place than the family dining room!

All of a sudden, the fury stopped. My dimpled little legs dropped to the floor and bolted for the kitchen. Tugging on my mother's apron, I exclaimed, "Mommy! Mommy! Guess what?"

"What?" she asked, anticipating some new flight of childish fancy, totally unrelated to the fiery keyboard drama I'd cut short in mid-combustion.

What I said she could never have predicted.

"Mommy," I exclaimed, breathless. "God's going to take all the bad people off the earth."

"He is?"

"Yep. They've been really awful and don't love Him. But, you know what?"

"No, what?"

"God's going to make a new place for everybody who loves Him, and they're going to go there. So it's going to be all right, isn't it?"

"Why, yes, sweetheart, it sure is."

And off I went, racing back to the piano to begin Act Two. No thunder and lightning this time. No earthquakes. Just caressing, flute-like sounds, probably a musical melange of every lullaby and every peaceful image contained in my almost three-year-old brain.

Decades later, my mother still tells this story. She tells it the same way every time. It stands complete, one cosmic moment crystallized and suspended in her memory. Until a few years ago, I disregarded her tale as pure fiction, a quaint piece of maternal nostalgia. Even if it were true, what was the point? Such a tiny, whimsical slice of my childhood couldn't possibly have any bearing on my life. Not surprisingly, I balked at worship ministry years later, unwilling to accept what my mother had known all along: God had chosen me to do something for His kingdom that involved both music and the Word. This was something quite beyond my experience or human capacity to accomplish. The struggle was on.

Perhaps you can relate to this struggle. Maybe you've covered your eyes from time to time, so that you won't see the hand of God upon you. Maybe you've stopped up your ears, so you can't hear God's clarion call on your life. Perhaps you were once commissioned as a worship leader. You became the "keeper of worship" and officially, you accepted a sacred charge. Inside, however, you were a bit unsure. Now, doubts are your daily bread. The thrill of beginning is gone. It's just Sunday to Sunday, program to program, and you're in a perpetual state of image-tweaking lest anyone find out you don't know what in the world you're doing up there on that platform.

I guarantee, you're not alone. Many of us as worship leaders reject God's anointing. We feel so undeserving, so utterly inadequate to the task God has assigned to us. We act like Moses. We cry out to God, "I'm not the one you want. I'm not a leader. I'm only a musician, and a mediocre one at that. You made a mistake!"

Ah, but God doesn't make mistakes. What's more, God doesn't choose people according to our standards.

We worship leaders would do well to memorize 1 Corinthians 1:26-29. "Think of what you were when you were called. Not many of you were wise by human standards; not many were influential; not many were of noble birth. But God chose the foolish things of the world to shame the wise; God chose the weak things of the world to shame the strong. He chose the lowly things of this world and the despised things—and the things that are not—to nullify the things that are, so that no one may boast before Him."

Who of us can accomplish anything apart from God's hand? Without God's grace, without God's empowering, refining Spirit, who could stand? Who could even think of ushering people into the magnificent presence of the One who is, was, and is to come—the omnipotent, omniscient, holy God who created, redeemed, and now sustains the very essence of life? Is there anyone who, in and of themselves, is truly fit to wear the mantle of worship leader, to mentor and mold the worship life of an entire congregation? Of course not. Yet, the news of the gospel is, God makes us sufficient. God does lavish, supernatural, beyond-imagining things through the unlikeliest of candidates...us.

Now, when my mother tells the story of that September day long ago, I listen. I marvel at how God speaks, even to almost-three-year olds. I remember my earliest lessons and my thrill at being asked to accompany the elementary school Christmas programs (yes, they actually had them, once upon a time!). I see myself as a twelve-year old, playing for nursing home sing-a-longs and county fair fashion shows. I replay all those nervous teen-age recitals, the contests won and lost. I see the rejection letter from the conservatory, ripped open and tossed on the floor. Then, my mind drifts to an arm injury right before college and three years of remedial practice. I feel the sting of humiliation as if it were yesterday, and see a defeated young woman, giving it all up, sealing her hope and her music books in a cardboard box. I hear the silence of the decade that followed. And I see that God was there, all the time. God still had a plan. I just needed to make myself available.

Brad Kauffman

Brad Kauffman is a graduate of Christ for the Nations Institute of Biblical Studies in Stony Brook, New York, where he studied theology and music theory. His heart and skills as a worship leader were developed under the guidance of then music director Martin Nystrom (Integrity Music recording artist). After a brief time on the mission field doing local church worship training he spent five years leading worship in churches in his home town of Lancaster, Pennsylvania. Brad also spent two years traveling with Dr. Michael Brown (author and leader in the Pensacola revival) overseas and throughout North America.

Raised in a godly home, Brad is the oldest of eight musical children (all the rest of whom are girls!) and is a singer, song writer, and keyboardist. He currently serves full-time as worship director for The Church of Grace and Peace in Toms River, New Jersey. For the past three years he has lead worship and overseen the music department, also leading the church's young adult's group.

Brad enjoys all types of sports, especially golfing, skiing and motorcycle riding. He also enjoys gardening.

The Mishaps of Ministry

———⌒⟁⌒———

Bryan McCrea, a friend of mine who had taken a new position as senior pastor of a growing congregation in a small town in Georgia, contacted me about coming down to lead worship for an area-wide meeting of churches he was putting together. Over ten years ago Bryan and I had graduated from the same Bible college together. As we said our good-byes on graduation day, preparing to head back to our different home states, we expressed how great it would be if one day the Lord would allow us to minister together. Now, as we talked on the phone, Bryan told me of his plan to have Dr. Michael Brown, a former Bible College professor of ours, come to Georgia and be the guest speaker for the special meeting. I smiled as the faded memory came to mind of our youthful plans for ministry together. The date for the meeting coincided with an opening in my schedule, and believing that God's blessing was on it, I quickly booked a flight.

We made arrangements to assemble a large choir, front-line singers, and a full band of musicians from different churches. I was to lead from the piano. We encountered some technical difficulties with the sound system during our rehearsal prior to the meeting but seemingly ironed them out right before the service started. The meeting began.

The moment we started the first song, I knew something was not right. The sound was drastically different than it was in our practice time. I simply could not hear things as before including the baby grand I was playing. I started to strike the keys harder in order to hear myself. At the same time the band was having noticeable difficulty following my lead. It didn't take long to realize that the monitor system was not on! We were left only with the sound coming from the guitar amps on stage and the very echoing house speakers high above and out in front of us. The sound engineer at the back of the auditorium seemed to be a mile away and oblivious to our dilemma on stage. All attempts to communicate with him failed, and I was left trying to signal with off-mic vocal instructions to the singers and musicians and at the same time pound my fingers even harder on the keys in between cues. It didn't take long before the drummer and I were out of sync. I kept trying to get him back in time with me by waving out the tempo with my left hand. Needless to say I was a bit distracted from focusing on God and leading the people in worship and began to become upset with what was happening.

Meanwhile, the congregation was enjoying themselves and entering into the presence of the Lord. I had to make a conscious effort to ignore the imperfections of the music and press in to what the Lord was really looking for—undivided worship. I finally felt like I broke through my own frustration and into worship, when in the middle of the last song suddenly the monitors came on much to the relief of the musicians and my now very sore fingers!

Just when I thought all mishaps for the evening were over my friend Bryan came to the pulpit to receive the evening offering. I was sitting there thinking of how proud I was of him for successfully calling together such a large group of ministers and churches all hungry for God to move in their area. But as he began to speak it became quickly evident that he had over-used his vocal chords during our worship time. With his voice almost gone he struggled to get his words out. Instead of cutting it short he continued on and on, choking out every word and getting softer and softer the longer he went. I soon began to feel sorry for him and couldn't help but clear my own throat in sympathy with his obvious discomfort. When I thought he had suffered enough embarrassment, I began to play the piano softly to give him a way out. He turned to me, choked out a very weak "Thanks Brad," released the ushers and sat down.

After the offering I took my seat on the platform next to Bryan who was given the honored seat next to the guest speaker. Seated on either side and behind us were about two dozen local pastors of the participating congregations. Michael jumped right into a stirring message and had just concluded his first point when the chair that Bryan was sitting on suddenly collapsed under him! His arms and legs went up in the air as body crashed loudly on the tile floor. Without missing a beat Michael turned and said, "You were supposed to wait until my second point to do that." The whole place erupted in laughter. What made it even more funny was that one of ministers had just given up that seat so Bryan could sit next to Michael. He was laughing so hard he had to go backstage to regain his composure.

In the end it was a meeting in which the Lord ministered to many hearts. After the sermon we went back to worshiping the Lord as Michael and Bryan began to pray for people at the altar for almost two hours. God's Spirit touched lives and set many free that night. The Lord showed me that polished perfection in our ministry efforts was not the stamp of His anointing. I learned once again not to lean on the arm of flesh or my own abilities, but rather on His ability to work even when things don't go exactly the way we plan them.

My Summer in St. Martin...

While attending Bible college as a full-time student, I was given the opportunity to extend my education another year with a local church/missions internship program. Realizing the benefits of this hands-on training and recognizing the call on my life to full-time ministry, I quickly agreed to continue my education. Many students felt their hearts being pulled toward particular places such as Africa, India, and Guatemala. I, on the other hand, had no such leaning. I told the faculty to send me wherever I was needed most. I must admit that I didn't complain when the place they chose for me turned out to be the beautiful Caribbean Island of St. Martin. Steve Bokmiller, a fellow student and friend of mine and I were to spend three months on the French side of the island working in a Black Pentecostal church to help the pastor in different areas of ministry, particularly in the area of worship.

Steve and I arrived and could hardly believe our fortune. We were to live with an indigenous family right across the street from the most gorgeous beach we had ever seen. We knew that some folks back home were questioning the validity of our "missions" endeavor, and at first, even I wondered how this would measure up to the sacrificial experiences of ministry I was sure the other students were going to have. We soon discovered that the local folks had very different diets than we were accustomed to. After being served fish heads, pig tail soup, and beef lungs and gravy, the old, wise missionary saying rang in my mind: "Don't say, 'Where You lead me I will follow,' unless you can say, 'What they feed me I will swallow'!"

Our first church service was quite an eye-opening event. The music leader started to sing and the people joined in. I was wondering where the musicians were. Slowly, one at a time, they showed up and went to their different instruments. The drummer, being the last one on the scene, showed up over a half-hour after the start of the service. To make matters worse, it didn't seem that the musicians were paying any attention to the song leader. Another thing that struck me as strange was that for 45 minutes we hadn't changed songs! It was a local song set to a reggae feel in which the leader would sing a line and the people would respond back. He would sing, "I tried the disco," and they would shout back "sowwa" (sour), "I tried the booze"—"sowwa," "I tried the dope" —"sowwa," and the big punch line chorus was "but my Jesus is sweeta. Oh yeah, my Jesus is sweeta." After 30 minutes Steve and I were looking at each other in disbelief. It took everything in us to keep from laughing when the pastor who was clapping and singing along leaned over to us and said with desperation in his voice, "I want new songs!"

It was not easy challenging the prevailing laid-back mentality of, "We'll do it tomorrow." However, with the pastor's full support we set out to teach the singers and musicians some new songs, principles of worship and practical ideas about how to work together as a team. We held rehearsals, classes, and private lessons and in the end saw some fruit from our labors. After months of working with these dear people, the whole worship team was coming together in unity, and even meeting prior to services for prayer. They were enjoying the new choruses and even added to them their own unique island rhythms. Without trying to change the local culture, the Lord showed us how to bring His people to a place of corporate worship in which they were edified and He was glorified. To this day I have a fond appreciation for different cultural styles of praise and worship, but I still haven't taken a liking to cow lungs!

Daniel Douma

Daniel Douma is a graduate of Christ for the Nations Institute in Dallas, Texas. He is a worship leader, musician and song writer who loves to lead people into the presence of God.

From 1991 through 1997 Daniel was the minister of music at the 2000-member Harvest Time Tabernacle in Fort Smith, Arkansas. He directed a choir of 100 voices along with a 30-piece orchestra.

For fun, Daniel collects wrist watches of all types. He also occasionally plays an adventure-filled round of golf.

Daniel currently resides in Fort Smith with his lovely wife, Kimberly, their daughter, Miriam, and son, Timothy.

My Music Library— Consecrated to Him

One day when I was digging through the mess I had created while enduring another Christmas musical, I decided to do some spring cleaning. I began to bring some order to the 500 CD's and more than 300 cassettes I had accumulated over the years. The vast majority of these (80%) were praise and worship recordings, I'm almost embarrassed to admit that I had so many. I'm certainly not rich. I just search out the demo sales, closeouts, etc., while earnestly praying for the best deals, and I will fight you for a "buy 4 get one free" sticker.

Why does a worship leader need so many recordings? First of all, I need to live a life of worship. I can't really do that even by listening to a local Christian music station. I must sit in communion with the Lord myself. I must know the holy of holies if I am to lead others there. So, besides worshiping on my own instrument, wherever I am, I am usually listening to a praise and worship recording.

Secondly, I view my recordings as a pastor might his book library. I am always able to find a fresh idea, a new song, or a new way to do a particular song. My college professor taught, "You've got to listen to all the great trumpet players so that you will glean from all of them in developing your own style." Listen only to recordings by one person and you'll begin to lead worship exactly like that person. That is okay, but we need a "you" more than we need a clone of someone else.

When I train other worship leaders, I ask them to listen to a selected recording each week. Through a questionnaire, they rate the worship leader in the area of flow, anointing, communication, song selection style, and voice quality. They list things they have learned and things they liked, as well as songs they did and didn't like. The last part of the questionnaire is an overall rating of the project. I have found this very effective to their growth as worship leaders.

Do I believe everyone must only listen to Christian music? I believe it is beneficial for all Christians, but for me as one with the awesome responsibility of leading people into His presence, it is *essential*. I have kept my promise to the Lord that no secular recordings will be in my possession. God unquestionably has the best ideas and songs to give. Contrary to popular belief, He doesn't give them to sinners first! Why would God reveal his musical ideas to an unsaved studio musician in L.A. before He would to a child of His who is worshiping Him?

Years ago, standing on a mountain in Missouri with Kimberly, my wife-to-be, I painfully did what the Lord had been speaking to me about for some time. I burned all my secular albums (remember they're those big flat vinyl things?!) that I had collected over the years. While praying together, Kimberly was convinced that because of my obedience the Lord would give me music from Him that I had never even dreamed of. I thought to myself, "Yeah, right." I had no thoughts of being a worship leader and writing worship songs for others to sing—I just played the trumpet in the band. But the Lord had a plan for me (just as He has for you) and has fulfilled His promise.

The recordings that I have found most helpful are those put out by individual churches, although I keep up with several major series such as Hosanna, Christ for the Nations, etc.

I encourage you to live a life in His presence. Listen to as many praise and worship recordings as possible. Worship Him one-on-one when you don't have to lead others. Make sure all your music listening pleases the Lord. I believe this will help you become all you can be for His glory!

Bob Sorge

Bob Sorge serves as the senior pastor of Zion Fellowship in Canandaigua, New York. He also manages Oasis House, a Christian book publisher. Bob's first book, Exploring Worship, has been widely acclaimed internationally by colleges and local church worship ministries as a practical textbook on praise and worship. Bob has recently written three other books, In His Face: A Prophetic Call to Renewed Focus, The Fire of Delayed Answers, and its sequel, The Fire of God's Love.

Bob's passion is to pursue the knowledge of Jesus Christ. In his "down time" he enjoys a recreational round of golf or ministering retribution with his chainsaw to the wood pile.

Bob and his wife, Marci, enjoy serving the Lord in Canandaigua, where they reside with their three children, Joel, Katie and Michael.

Worship Is No Sweat

———⟡———

It was over a decade ago that I attended my first worship conference. I still remember the sense of awe I felt as I experienced a form and depth of worship that was entirely new for me.

I came home from that conference with my eyes nearly popping out with vision for what God could do in and through the worship life of my home church.

My church knew immediately that I was different. There was a new passion, a new intensity—and also a form of expression that was new to our church. My zeal to see change was graciously tolerated for a year. Then came the confrontation.

The pastor called me into his office and told me the elders had talked about my worship leading. They had all agreed that they didn't like the way things were going and that I needed to make some changes. I was young and inexperienced, and deeply mortified at the chastisement.

So I approached the elders on an individual basis. I asked what they perceived to be the problem, and what I should do about it. Each one gave me a totally different answer! "Not enough hymns." "Too many fast songs." "We're in a rut." I came away with my head swimming and cried out, "Lord, what is going on here?"

Then the Lord helped me to see the common denominator in all the elders' responses as He spoke gently to my heart: "You're striving in the flesh." I realized that I had succumbed to using my natural strengths in trying to implement a godly vision. I was definitely being drawn forward by the Spirit, but in my zeal to see the people enter into the freshness of what God was doing, I had begun to push on the thing with my soul.

The Lord began to teach me how to release a worship service to Him and not get all uptight about whether it was meeting my expectations. To bring me to a place of balance, the Lord actually had to get me to the place where I didn't really care at all about how the worship service went—I just put my eyes on Jesus and enjoyed Him and left the worship service up to Him. I discovered it worked. The people still worshiped, even when I took a less aggressive posture. Whereas I used to come away from leading a worship service with my shirt soaking, it was during this time that I learned that "worship is no sweat."

I still have to release to the Lord every worship service I lead. How I long to see a dynamic release of praise and worship in the congregation, but I've learned to take my hands off the service and surrender to the genuine prompting of the Holy Spirit. I've continued to grow in this ever since that time about twelve years ago when my pastor took on the willingness to confront.

Monty Kelso

Monty Kelso has been director of creative communication and worship leader for Coast Hills Community Church in Aliso Viejo, California, since its beginning in the mid-80s. As well as leading a dynamic creative team at Coast Hills (a Willow Creek Association church), he is a worship leader for Maranatha! Music and continues to lead one of Maranatha's Worship Leader Workshop teams. He regularly participates in various conferences throughout the U.S. as a worship leader and conference speaker.

A passion for effective teams that creatively communicate Jesus Christ through the arts is evident whether you attend the Coast Hills Creative Communications conference, one of Monty's workshops, talk to him on the phone, or read his articles found in Worship Leader magazine.

Monty sums up his life by saying, "It's all about relationships—finding ways to help others (and myself) continue to grow and enjoy relationship with God, family, the church family, and people in general."

Monty, his wife, Christa, and their three sons, Conner, Trevor and Bryson, live in Laguna Beach, California.

Getting a Grip On Letting Go

When my wife and I helped launch this new church plant called Coast Hills Community Church twelve years ago, I was young, without children, mildly experienced and ready to tackle just about anything of a pioneering nature. Especially when "the call" required that we move to the beach and settle in San Clemente, California (whose license plate frames read: "World's Best Climate"). The idea of starting a new church unencumbered by the web of former staff and tradition was a long time dream. Finally a place where my passion for creative worship could be realized. Add to this ideal situation the fact that the senior pastor and his wife, Denny and Leesa Bellesi, shared this same dream. In fact, Leesa was a seasoned dancer and choreographer, and Denny was a product of Youth For Christ and two of the most creative churches in Southern California. Needless to say we had vision far beyond our initial capacity. Here we were a start-from-scratch, interdenominational community church with little financial support and only a handful of enthusiastic people. What we did have going for us was the right people at the right time in the right place and a Mighty God who desired to build His church in the growing community of South Orange County California.

Like many other church plants our "portable church" set up camp at a local high school. Every Sunday morning at daybreak a team of able-bodied volunteers would transform Dana Hills High School in Dana Point into a sanctuary of worship. Volunteers set up class rooms for the children, sound and lighting systems, staging, signs, refreshments and 300 feet of curtains that tied on to the second story railing encompassing our meeting "hall." Volunteers showed up every Sunday to play, sing, act, hang visuals, usher, greet, serve donuts and host the information center. It was my job to see that all this happened without a hitch each week.

From the beginning we placed a high value on communicating with excellence and authenticity and that value spread to every fiber of the church. We worked hard to insure that this value was reflected everywhere you looked. I was personally driven to give God our best no matter the cost. This drive not only reflected in the product of worship but also in the process. My week was soon filled up with countless meetings leading volunteers down this new path of contemporary worship. I then thought I knew exactly how things should be done. After all, I saw the big picture and was the only one who could possibly know the right way to make things happen. The grip I held on my ministry was strengthening as I saw empty chairs filling up over the rapidly passing months. I figured we must have been doing this right because people kept coming.

It wasn't that I did everything myself. I had put together a creative planning team within the first year of ministry. I had identified point leaders for each of the teams. I even left for six weeks within the first year to do an overseas ministry project. It seemed that all was going well, the way God had intended. After all, He was blessing my hard work with a growing church and growing ministry team. There was no denying that Coast Hills had my signature all over it. My dreams were being realized.

Fast-forward seven years. It was the early nineties. My wife and I had managed to find time to start our family. The church had grown significantly to three services and we were rapidly outgrowing the high school. I had squeezed out of the general budget enough money to hire a part-time music director and a part-time assistant but was still holding a tight grip on the details of what was then called, the Celebration Arts ministry. The time had come for Coast Hills to find its own permanent location and quickly the pursuit began. Meanwhile, the demands of programming and rehearsing every week's service was ever before us. By now there was a host of other special events and projects added to the annual diet of this entre-preneur-led church. It's accurate to say that at this point most of us were, by our own initiative, overworked and under-paid and loving every minute of it. The lack of material resources was compensated by a wealth of human resources with talent that surpassed anyone's wildest expectations. This may have been the very factor that set me up for the big "shut down" to come.

In 1993 after two years of praying, planning, praying, capital campaigns, designing buildings and praying some more, we, by God's grace, squeaked into our new 1500 seat auditorium in Aliso Viejo. It was designed as a community theater in an effort to build a bridge between the arts community and the church. What we hadn't planned on was that the major budget cut-backs at the eleventh hour of construction would impact mostly the auditorium audio-visuals. With the exception of some expensive wiring and a bare-bones lighting system, we were reduced to a road weary sound system and an unlimited supply of duct tape. Yet the expectation fostered by this magnificent new building left both the congregation and the community waiting for the *next level* of dynamic communication. No pressure!!!

After years of hoping and dreaming for our own building and all the solutions it would bring to our never ending complexities of being a portable church, it suddenly became the very catalyst that would lead me to the end of myself.

It was a combination of several factors that are continually becoming clearer to me that nearly drove my team and me over the edge. I realize now that nearly all of them are rooted in the sin of pride. A relentless pursuit of excellence that not only was a positive reflection of God's church but also a positive reflection on me kept me driving forward no matter how steep the climb. My identity and source of gratification became the successes of the Celebration Arts ministry. In some ways my ministry became my god. I worshiped the successes along the way. I found great satisfaction in a plan that worked. I had confused who the object of my worship was.

The defining moment was on an ordinary weekend when I realized that my ability to worship God was totally conditional. My personal satisfaction level of the service determined it. How profound was the flow of the service? What was the performance quality of the artists? Was the technician's execution of the plan flawless? Anything less then perfection left me frustrated, depressed and unable to worship God authentically.

Not only was God offended with these offerings of "filthy rags," but also it had become clear to my team that I cared much more about the "product" than I cared about them. My grip on the ministry was so tight that even though I delegated responsibility, I didn't trust. Even though I included others, I didn't value their input. Even though I ran things by them, I still did what I wanted to do. What's ironic is that, for the most part, what I "went to the mat" over was all worthwhile and under healthy circumstances the right thing. After all, we were pioneering a new model church that received its fair share of criticism. It was easy to justify my actions for the sake of the cause. I had a way of making anyone who disagreed with me second-guess his or her conviction and leave the conversation confused and frustrated. This only fostered hostility in those few with whom I worked most closely.

In an effort to cope with the extreme stress of this season of our still growing church and a leader that was on a road to destruction, they began to talk amongst themselves and compare notes. As you can imagine, perceptions were embellished and my shortcomings were intensified. This was not a happy camp!

To the credit of my long-time pastor and partner in ministry a meeting was called. Denny had invited any and everyone involved in leadership within the realm of my ministry to his house to get to the root of all the layers of stuff that had been accumulating over the previous months.

I'll never forget that August evening in 1993 when about 15 people gathered together to lovingly confront me as they saw me on the verge of spinning out and becoming another ministry casualty. It was that painful process of hearing the perceptions and feelings of those that I had gone to battle with that I began to realize my controlling behavior. It was in those few focused minutes that God convicted me of my sin. It was in that moment of brokenness that God showed me that I cared far too much about the organization of the church and its mission, vision and values. I cared far too little about the things that mattered most: to love God with all my heart, soul, mind, and strength and to love others more than myself. It was at that moment I committed to loosen the grip I had had on my ministry and to learn to serve those that I lead even when it means letting people or programs fail.

Today, when I worship God there is a profound appreciation of His grace. Whether I worship Him privately or publicly, I am reminded that He is most pleased when I offer Him my best, derived from a pure heart. A heart that is holy and blameless before Him. A heart that holds things loosely because I know that God is in charge. I now know that more than any model, program, plan, or production...people matter the most!

Scott C. Smith

Scott Smith is currently the worship and arts pastor at Bethel Temple in Hampton, Virginia. For 10 years he traveled across the United States and Canada with his family and other ministry teams. In 1989 Scott moved to Southern California where he became the minister of music at the Eagle's Nest in Irvine, California, for eight years.

Scott has recorded four praise and worship recordings and has produced recordings for several other artists and churches. He utilizes a mobile studio based at his church.

Along with Karry Godwin, Scott developed "Contemporary Concepts for Guitar and Bass," a one-hour teaching video for guitar and bass.

In 1997 Scott, his wife, Priscilla, and their children, Dezrik and Samuel, moved to Hampton, Virginia, where they now reside.

Some Trust in Sound Systems and Some in Synthesizers

After traveling across America as well as several other nations around the world, I have come to appreciate all the wonderful tools and resources we have to help us in our worship in this country. I often wonder if our zeal for leading our congregations into praise and worship would diminish if our sound mix was not right, or we did not have quality microphones, or the latest in keyboard technology. Too many times we allow the "tools" of worship to stand in the way of sincere, honest, heart-felt worship.

Sadly enough, I was present at one service where a worship leader would not accept what he was given as monitors and stormed off the platform. As he departed he made certain the audio crew knew what he thought of them. Jokingly, the rest of us astonished musicians said, "Now we can really worship!"

There have been times in the past when a very gifted worship leader did not show up and I had to lead with half the band. The truth is that those have been some of the most awesome times of worship. Why? Because we were forced not to rely on the "tools" of worship leading but instead were focused totally on the Lord. I believe that is why so many foreign countries have some of the most powerful worship experiences. It is because they don't rely on talent, or sound systems, or all of the other things in which we so often put our trust. They have learned that the most important factor in worship leading is the attitude of the heart.

After being in full-time ministry now for 18 years, I have learned one very important thing: if God can use me, He can use anyone! As I have traveled, I have frequently been asked, "What is your formal training?" The truth is I only went to school through the eighth grade. From that point on I traveled for about ten years ministering in churches with my family. During those years on the road I played bass guitar and occasionally piano (in the keys of C, F, and on a good day B-flat!). Somewhere in the middle of one of my tours I took the test for my GED and passed. That's the extent of my formal training.

When I was hired by a church in 1989, my job was to lead the choir and lead worship. In retrospect I find this original church position quite humorous because I really was not interested in being a choir director, and, at the time, I thought a worship leader just led some cute little choruses. After about two months in my new position, all three of our piano players/keyboardists left the church! And, of course, I got the call, "Scott you will now be lead-ing worship...from the piano!" My weakness at the piano was highlighted when I tried to sing while playing. At times it was awful. To make matters worse, the drummer, who had just started playing a few months prior, would sometimes accidently reverse the kick and snare on a fast two-beat song. You guessed it: *train wreck!!* I had first heard the term, "warfare praise" about that time. I knew that's what I was experiencing, but it wasn't a battle in the heavenlies. It was a battle on the platform!

Although I was pretty distraught over the situation at the time, I see how God used that to get me where I am today. The Lord apparently has quite a sense of humor, doesn't He? The interesting thing about my beginning experiences as a worship leader—and all of the accompanying sweat and tears—is that God used those things to take the performance mentality out of me. The Lord was always so faithful as I struggled in my weakness. *He* became my strength!

There were many times that I wondered about the wisdom of God's choice of me as a worship leader. I frequently wondered, "Why me, Lord?" However, after nearly every service that I thought I had bungled, He always brought someone to me to give me the encouragement I needed to go on. I learned that it is not our gifts that make us of service to God. It's the attitude of our hearts and the desire to please the Father with what He has entrusted us to do.

"Look to the LORD and his strength; seek his face always" (1 Chronicles 16:11). That's my desire. No matter what level my gift is at right now, my first priority is to look to the Lord and His strength—to seek His face. My heart yearns for His presence! I encourage you to do what I have found most effective in developing my gift: spend time with God. Know Him. Rely on Him. Far more than formal training, these are the really important things.

Charlie & Jill LeBlanc

Charlie and Jill LeBlanc have pursued the call of God on their lives to teach, encourage, and inspire by the Word of God through song (based on Colossians 3:16), along with leading congregations all over the world into God's presence through praise and worship.

Beginning their adventure into full-time ministry in 1980, the LeBlancs have fulfilled the spectrum of church staff positions ranging from worship leader, associate pastor and youth pastor. Since 1985 until now, they have traveled extensively ministering through music and the Word. Presently, they are the worship leaders for all of the Joyce Meyer Ministries conferences, which has been a great avenue to reach many more people.

Charlie and Jill have recorded six CDs of their own using mostly their own original songs. Included are a live praise and worship series, and their latest release, a Christmas album entitled, "The Little Child." Additionally, Charlie was the worship leader on two of Integrity's Hosanna! recordings, "Lord of All" and "To Him Who Sits On the Throne." Both Charlie and Jill have been song writers for and sung background vocals on several of Integrity's earlier recordings.

The LeBlancs live in St. Louis, Missouri, with their three children Camille, Cherrie and Beau. They are members of St. Louis Family Church.

The Heart of the Matter

Several years ago Jill and I were serving as worship leaders at a growing church in St. Louis, Missouri. During that time we experienced a great lesson in worship leading that has helped us to this day.

One afternoon, the pastor came into my office to share an exciting vision he had: to rent a large auditorium and combine both of our Sunday morning services into one big, explosive gathering of all of the saints. We would call it "Super Sunday." As he continued to share his ideas of bringing in a special musical guest, and possibly a drama presentation, I began to catch the vision. We continued to discuss all of the preparations that I would need to handle, including special songs to teach the band and worship singers, and special practices for this great event. The work began with only one month lead time, so we worked very hard, planning and preparing continually.

Over the next few weeks the details were coming together in extraordinary ways. The entire worship team was excited about the special service, and my wife, Jill, and I were preparing our hearts for a really special time in leading God's people in worship.

The great day arrived after weeks of intense rehearsing. The band, singers, and sound crew all arrived at the auditorium very early for final sound checks. We all were excited and ready to go!

As was our custom, we met backstage for prayer and worship together about a half hour before the service started. I was a little nervous, since I had not seen the pastor yet. He normally would be there early with us, giving his last minute suggestions and encouragement to the group, and then would join us in prayer. Nevertheless, we entered into a time of prayer and heartfelt praise together, as the clock ticked all the way down to starting time.

The noise in the auditorium and a sneak peak every now and then proved that the room was rapidly filling up with not only our congregation from both Sunday services, but also their friends and relatives. The place was jam packed! Just as we said our, "Amen," I saw the pastor walk in. Little did I know at the time that he had spent half the night in the hospital emergency room with a serious problem.

When pastor and I finally connected that morning, he shared about the excitement in his heart regarding the service and asked if everything was ready. "Everything's great!" I responded. He asked if Jill and I were ready to lead the people in praise and worship. I assured him that we were as prepared as we could be. (Are any of us ever *really* totally ready to lead in worship of the Almighty Creator?!) Pastor then informed me that he would simply open the service, greet the people, and turn it right over to us for leading the praise and worship.

As we all got into our places with instruments and microphones in hand, our pastor approached the podium to open the service. There was an obvious excitement among the people. Upon pastor's first greeting of, "Isn't the Lord's presence wonderful in this place?!", everyone present erupted in praise and applause for the King of kings and Lord of lords. The faith and expectancy in the room was almost tangible! Sensing that the people were definitely ready to worship, our pastor responded by opening up with a song that he couldn't contain any longer: "Then sings my soul, my Savior God to Thee, how great Thou art, how great Thou art!" The congregation joined in with glorious worship from their hearts. It was so intense that it seemed as though even the angels had joined in with us!

When the chorus ended, another enormous eruption of praise broke out. Jill and I stood just behind the pastor and off to the side, with microphones in hand, raring to go like a couple of race horses. All of the wonderful new songs and the great band licks we had practiced were being rehearsed in my head as I waited for him to signal us to come and take over. As the presence of the Lord powerfully filled the room, our pastor spontaneously took off into, "We bring the sacrifice of praise..." with the band running to catch up. Before I knew it, everyone in the place seemed to be worshiping... everyone except me. With a half-cocked smile on my face, I began to realize that something wasn't right on the inside of me. All these weeks of preparing to lead worship this special morning was all-of-a-sudden being taken away from me in an instant. I knew my heart was wrong, so in the midst of this celebration, the Lord and I had a little conversation.

"Lord, I know my heart is wrong, I need your help."

"Charlie, why did you come here this morning?"

"To lead your people into worship, and to worship You myself, Lord."

"Well, are the people worshiping?"

"Yes, Lord. But..."

He stopped me and said, "Then the mission is accomplished. Now, you just get your heart right and begin to worship Me."

This was a very difficult lesson to learn. You see, it really doesn't matter who is leading the worship. What matters is that we all worship Him!

After that experience, a new level of freedom came into my life, a new joy to serve and help people come into God's presence, no matter what the situation might be. If I can help in any way, whether it be preparing the worship team, playing an instrument, singing background vocals, or leading the worship, it makes no difference. Just as long as the mission is being accomplished and God's people worship Him in spirit and truth (John 4:24).

Perhaps we should all make a new commitment to humble ourselves and submit to one another, preferring one another, and serving each other, to see God's praises fill the earth.

Dave Michael Bell

Composer of worship standards, "Shout, Shout for Joy," "Magnificent God" and "There Is no Other Name," Dave Michael Bell carries a special passion for leading people into the Lord's presence. Dave Michael and his band have traveled extensively conducting worship concerts and conference events in the U.S., Mexico and Japan.

Dave Michael is currently working on his fifth worship recording, to be released in January of 1999. His two latest releases, "Lion of Judah" and "Prince of Peace," have received worldwide distribution by Word, Inc. "Lion of Judah" was released in English, Spanish and French. Dave Michael's current thrust in worship ministry is one of "turning generation X'ers into Xtreme worshipers."

Dave Michael oversees the worship and music ministry of Revival Temple in San Antonio, Texas. His area of ministry consists of four worship teams, choir and orchestra, as well as worship musician development and mentoring programs. He also oversees Dancing Heart Music, a worship music recording and publishing company and training center for musicians, worship leaders, record producers and engineers.

Dave Michael presently lives in San Antonio with his wife, Jodi, and five sons, Matthew, Michael, Mark, Micah and Mitchell.

The Stuff Trap

It was 2:15 A.M. All was quiet throughout the house. I had just spent the whole day with my band, preparing for a short tour. We had done some rehearsing, fine-tuned our equipment, and tied down those seemingly endless logistical "loose ends" that always seem to manifest at the last minute. The entire team (14 folks) was unified, ready, and excited to be leaving early the next morning. I was just turning in for the night, tired, but satisfied, when...WHAM!...the Holy Spirit began to work me over.

As I walked through our living room to turn out a light, I spotted my son's Bible on a nearby table. The Lord (now, *that* is an unmistakable voice!) said, "Pick up the Bible and read it!"

I replied, "Lord, it's late, and I've been preparing all day." With even more urgency, I heard again in my spirit, "Read it now!"

"OK" I replied. "What do you want me to read?"
His reply, clear, and unmistakable was "Obadiah 4."

Obadiah? I knew Obadiah was one of the minor prophets of the Old Testament but this was certainly not a book I had spent lots of time studying in-depth.

While turning to the passage I thought, "The Lord wants to encourage me one last time today...to affirm our efforts and to build confidence in my spirit with a little Scripture as I retire for the night." Little did I realize that the next few moments would spawn a life change in me and members of my team.

The fourth verse of Obadiah reads, "'Though you ascend as high as the eagle, and though you set your nest among the stars, from there I will bring you down,' says the LORD."

After I read this passage, I closed the Bible and muttered, "Well, Lord, I guess I didn't hear You correctly," still thinking that the Lord was trying to encourage me and believing that this verse could not possibly be connected with me in any way. Immediately, I heard His voice clearly saying, "This is the correct passage. Read it again."

Upon the second reading of this verse the Holy Spirit began a work of conviction in my heart. I started to weep and told the Lord that if this verse was describing me, then I had no business ministering to the people of God in worship...or even to the lost!

I asked the Lord to show me how I was exalting myself. At once, I felt conviction for putting so much emphasis on all of the stuff—yes, stuff—which so often seems required for a "full blown" worship event. What I'm talking about is stuff like our instruments and rigs, sound equipment, staging, MIDI computer systems, effects, vehicles, lights, and even our new songs with their "trick" arrangements.

As He convicted me, I began to realize that even while we may be quoting John 3:30 ("He must increase, but I must decrease") we are exalting ourselves when we spend our quality time pursuing the accumulation and improvement of our stuff. He wants us to make our relationship with Him our highest priority. He is the source of all that we do, not our stuff!

The Lord further pierced my soul by asking, "Dave, would you and your band be willing to leave all of your instruments and equipment on the truck, and go in and minister with the instruments you find in the host church?" and "If I led you and your team not to sing any of your songs, but just to minister in Word and in prayer, would you do it?"

I wept, repented, and wept some more. I asked the Lord to forgive me for allowing stuff to use up quality time that should have been spent on my knees with Him. I asked Him to forgive me for relying so heavily on our equipment, musical abilities, and human creativity. I also asked the Lord for the grace to approach my team with these issues. I was determined that we would never minister out of a spirit laced with even a hint of what I saw highlighted in Obadiah 4.

As I repented, I felt the Lord cleansing my heart from what was actually a form of idolatry. I am so thankful for

His marvelous grace! The next morning I approached my team with these issues and saw a most incredible miracle: God had been dealing with several of them in exactly the same manner! Together, we determined never to fall into the "stuff trap" again.

God has given us wonderful equipment, but we must never "worship" the equipment. We must never build up ourselves by thinking that we are improving the essence of our effectiveness by adding more "gear" or "trick" arrangements. In submission to Him, we must walk and minister in obedience and humility. Jesus must be our product, our target of exaltation, and that which we give to those to whom we minister. Jesus is the answer, not some awesome new MIDI system or lighting gimmick!

Since that very memorable day when God dealt with my heart, our tours and ministry events have been characterized by an increasing sense of being "broken" before the Lord. While we continue to take our instruments and gear, our hearts are turned toward Jesus, not the stuff! Even though the lesson of Obadiah 4 was quite hard for me to take, I am thankful that God cares enough about us to chasten us and cause us to change. I am a changed man as a result of His conviction and mercy.

Tommy Walker

Tommy Walker is currently the worship leader at Christian Assembly Foursquare Church in Los Angeles, California. He has written such songs as "Mourning Into Dancing" from Ron Kenoly's Hosanna! Music recording, "Lift Him Up" and "Lord, I Believe In You" from Crystal Lewis' latest release "Gold."

He has been the key worship leader for Promise Keeper stadium events, Greg Laurie Harvest Crusades, Luis Palau's El Paso, Texas, 1997 Crusade and many others. Tommy has written songs for these crusades such as "No Greater Love," "These Things Are True of You" and wrote the new chorus arrangement of the great hymn "A Mighty Fortress Is Our God" which was sung at Promise Keepers' "Stand In The Gap" in Washington D.C. He recorded a live CD for Maranatha Music in 1994 and has written and sung many other songs for them as well.

Tommy is currently involved in taking worship evangelism to various parts of the world with the C.A. Worship Band (Christian Assembly) leading people to Christ, giving to the poor and training worship leaders throughout the world. He has also recorded four CDs for his church's independent label "Get Down Records."

You Can Do It, Tommy

⎯⎯⎯⎯⎯

I'm the last of six kids in my family, all of whom were somewhat musical. I, however, pursued music with a passion my whole life. Because of this, I was given opportunities to lead worship in different youth groups at a very young age. However, I usually found I was extremely nervous—the kind of nervous that makes everyone else nervous and definitely can hinder worship.

Then one day as I was talking to my mom. She told me something I've never forgotten. She said, "Tommy, throughout my whole pregnancy with you I prayed every day that God would give me a musician, someone who would give glory to God through music." I know it sounds simple, but what this said to me was that God created me for this. Before I was even born, He was knitting in me abilities to usher people into His presence.

I think a number one enemy of worship leaders is a lack of confidence. This is certainly an issue I have had to deal with continually. The way I've begun to overcome this problem is by letting God tell me something I heard Him say after talking to my mom. "You can do this, Tommy. I created you for this."

One instance I'll never forget was in May of 1997. I was given the incredible and undeserved privilege of leading a stadium full of men at a Promise Keepers event. As I was walking onto the stage I remember feeling terrified and thinking, "This is definitely over my head. How did I ever get myself into this?" I quickly quoted one of my favorite verses (1 Peter 2:9) and whispered it in the first person to myself. "I'm a chosen person, in a royal priesthood and part of a holy nation. I belong to God that I might declare His praises."

After I prayed that, God whispered those words to me again, "You can do this, Tommy. I created you for this." After the first song was counted off and we got things rolling, a joy came over me that was so deep I could hardly breathe. I couldn't help but picture my mom sitting in a rocking chair praying for me as I was still in her womb.

Letting God remind me that He chose me and He put these abilities in me has enabled me to do things far beyond what I could have ever dreamed, and in the process, I've been able to give Him even more glory wherever He has taken me!

The Stopping Question: What If I Must?

—⟨≪≫⟩—

I was recently in the Philippines doing what we call a "Worship Evangelism Concert" and experienced something they never taught me in worship leader school. What do you do if the crowd won't let you end the song? This is a good problem to have.

At our gathering, the people were joyfully clapping along with the rhythm of the song. Every time I tried to end, they wouldn't stop clapping. Basically what I learned that night was, if something is working and ministering, don't stop. We repeated the song in every way possible for about twenty minutes, taking instrumental solos, singing it a capella, etc. It was an incredible time! If I had stopped the song when planned, the momentum we gained through that experience would have been no where as great.

Many years ago I had a similar situation that went the other direction. I was leading worship at my church and started a song in much too high a key. The song had a big range, so everyone knew when we got to the chorus that it was going be all over. You have to understand this was a ballad in the midst of what was supposed to be a serious moment. Well, me in my lack of experience thought I should pretend everything was cool and just go for it. When the chorus came, my voice cracked and I couldn't even come close to reaching the high notes, much less expect the congregation to hit those notes. Everyone finally just started laughing. Of course, I had my eyes closed pretending there was no problem. When I opened them I realized they were basically laughing at me.

What I learned from this worship disaster was to loosen up a little bit and fix something early on before it is too late. Since then I've made the same mistake but quickly changed the key before the chorus or just stopped the song altogether and simply told everyone what I was doing and started it up again. The moral to this story is that if something isn't working, don't keep going and make people suffer through it. It's much better to stop and begin again.

Darlene Zschech

Darlene Zschech has made music an integral part of her life since she was a child. From the age of 10 she performed in a weekly children's television show, singing, dancing and hosting segments. As a teenager Darlene continued in music fronting various gospel bands in Brisbane, Australia.

With considerable session experience, Darlene has worked on numerous commercials. Some of her most often played include commercials for McDonald's, Special "K," KFC and Diet Coke.

A proficient song writer, Darlene's most well-known song is "Shout to the Lord." It was nominated for song of the year for the 1998 Dove Awards. Her album by the same title was nominated for album of the year for the 1997 Dove Awards.

Darlene is lead vocalist, worship leader and co-producer of Hillsongs Australia's best-selling albums, "God is in the House," "All Things are Possible," and the newly-released "Touching Heaven, Changing Earth."

For the past 12 years Darlene and her husband, Mark, have been a vital part of the leadership team at Hills Christian Life Centre in Sydney, Australia. Darlene is the worship pastor and oversees the creative ministries department.

257

Praise through Pain
Adapted from the book,
Worship - Hillsongs Australia Leadership Series

Some time ago I was leading worship at a church in Texas. During the service my attention was drawn to a particular young couple who were visibly basking in the presence of God. Throughout the worship their faces were radiant. They seemed to be worshiping God with everything they had. I knew even then that I had to meet them. I was interested to know what caused such fervent worship of God.

When we did meet I asked them about their love for God. I wanted them to share something of their testimony with me. As they began, they held hands and related how just six weeks earlier they had lost their five-week-old baby to crib death. That was certainly not what I was expecting to hear!

They were living, breathing testimonies of Exodus 15:2: "The Lord is my strength and my song." Their faith and worship were a declaration of God's power and lordship over their lives. Through their attitude of praise, God was able to minister to them and hold their lives together.

I will never forget this family. Their testimony and uncompromising faith in God has stirred and challenged the lives of many Christians. We are created to worship.

However, it is not always easy when your world seems to be falling apart. When we start to sing and praise God, we are choosing to lay aside the problems of our lives. Instead, we lift our voices and our hearts to the One Who ultimately holds our lives in His hands.

I clearly remember one morning just after my father passed away. I was hanging out the wash (some things in life just never change!!) and my heart was breaking. My father was a wonderful man, and even though I knew he was now dancing with the angels, I missed him so much I found it hard to breathe. Because of this I started to sing, just quietly to myself, "To God be the glory..." (one of my father's favorite songs). I sensed the presence of God envelope me anew. There while I was standing in my yard with my two-year-old running around by my feet, the Lord was touching my life. There was a wonderful healing in my heart that day.

Melodies and music have a dynamic ability to involve your soul, to connect with your heart, emotions and mind. There is a power for life that is found only as we set our focus on the Lord and worship Him.

Bob Kilpatrick

Few contemporary Christian praise songs make it to the "classic" category. At least two of Bob Kilpatrick's songs are there: "Lord Be Glorified" and "Here Am I (Send Me To The Nations)." Though these songs keep popping up on the "greatest hits" lists, there are many other tunes for which Bob is known: "Won By One," "I Am Yours," "Tell Me The Story" and "I Will Not Be Ashamed" among them.

Bob might be called a Christian music veteran. He has been in full-time music ministry since 1976. Over the years he has shared the stage with a veritable ministry "Who's Who" including Dr. Jack Hayford, Dr. Lloyd John Ogilvie, Corrie Ten Boom, Michael W. Smith, dcTalk, Tony Campolo, Pat Boone, Anne Graham Lotz, Jars of Clay, Keith Green and Andraé Crouch.

These days, besides traveling all over the world, Bob leads the Making Music Ministry seminars, heads up a non-profit ministry organization and is the president of two record labels, Fair Oaks Music and TPG (Think. Pray. Groove.) Records. He is still married to Cindy, his high school girlfriend. Together they have five children and live in Fair Oaks, California.

Listening to Ray Sing

⸺◈⸺

"When I was a young boy, back on Orange Street,
I used to sit by my classroom window and dream,
Then go home and listen to Ray sing,
I believed in my soul, after school..."

If you recognize these words from the "No Guru, No Method, No Teacher" album, you're a true Van Morrison fan. If you've heard his music, you know that he listened very closely while Ray sang. No one can miss the effect Ray Charles' voice had on the young Morrison.

How it happened can be a mystery, though. As far as we know, Ray never visited the teenage Van in school in Great Britain. He didn't give him personal instruction how to bend notes, play with a lyric or voice a phrase. Yet, there is the unmistakable influence in his voice.

This mystery—how one passes on knowledge, character and passion—is on my mind. I have had a hand in mentoring several up-and-coming Christian musicians in the last few years. One of them, Justin Fox, is single-handedly responsible for it.

Justin came to me four years ago asking to do a summer internship with me as a requirement for his college graduation. He drove three hours to spend an hour with me and only asked about interning in a general way at the very end of our conversation. He said something like, "Have you ever, like, uh, considered, uh, say, having, like, an intern?" I told him that it had possibly crossed my mind in the last, oh, twenty years, but I couldn't remember when exactly. He said "Cool!" and "Sweet!" and was gone.

The next thing I knew, the college was on the phone wanting the details of my "Internship Program." Into the deep end from the high dive!

Justin and Heidi, his bride of two weeks, did come for the summer. And stayed on. We produced two albums for him. I taught him everything I know about talking to youth pastors, and pastors (don't say "Cool!" and "Sweet!"), concertizing, song writing and recording. I took him with me to concerts. I encouraged him to get out there himself. I threw him into the deep end a couple of times myself.

Justin and Heidi now live in Southern California with their two year old daughter, Farrah. He's working on his fourth album, singing around the world, has a sponsorship from World Vision and his college alma mater and is doing very nice work. And you know what? People tell me they can hear my influence in Justin.

Van got it from Ray. Justin got it from Bob. For good or for bad, how did that happen? I think we can find a model in the relationship between Jesus and His group of disciples.

Aside from the more obvious differences, there was one striking dissimilarity between Jesus' approach and the contemporary rabbinical system of education. In the

Jewish tradition, a divinity student studied at the feet of an older venerated rabbi whose doctrine was attractive to him. After the student graduated, he hung out his shingle proclaiming that he taught the "____ School of Thought." Thereby, he attracted students to his teaching. What mattered most was not who he was but what he taught.

Jesus, in distinct contrast, called disciples to Himself. He said "follow *Me*," "come to *Me*," "*I* am the Way." Jesus put the emphasis on Himself, not His teachings. His disciples didn't go to classes or do homework (that we know of, but don't use this argument with your parents). They weren't graded, didn't march the aisle in a graduation ceremony or hang a certificate on their office walls. What they did do was to spend day and night, week after week for three and a half years with Jesus. They must have talked about everything. They probably asked questions ("What exactly did you pray over those loaves and fishes?" "What do you want us to do with the leftovers?").

They spent time watching Jesus live His life. He sent them out two by two (the equivalent of being thrown in the deep end). He got angry in front of them. He cried. He talked to God in public. He made sudden unexplained changes in their plans. He healed hurting people. He got them in big trouble with the government. And then He left them. And that, boys and girls, is the foundation for the Church today.

Is that how you would have begun your Church here on earth if you were God? Me neither. But that's how Jesus did it, because He knows something important. People make a stronger bond with people than they do with ideologies. Jesus called them (and us) to Himself because He wanted them (and us) committed to Himself, not His philosophy. He calls us to spend time with, to bond to, to watch and to learn from Him.

As a bona fide Mentor, I have tried to explain to my bona fide Mentees about the disappointments that accompany this lifestyle. I have told my disciples about the potholes and the pitfalls. Many times, my talking has been to no avail. Why? Not because I didn't make myself clear. They just need to see it lived. So our "Internship Program" that Justin Fox initiated for us is not primarily a classroom situation. Most of our training happens at concerts, in the studio and in our offices. What would happen in a classroom for others takes place at Starbucks for us. Life is good.

We call it the CrossWalk Music Family. There are several reasons behind the name. We're not a label, though we sometimes act like one. We're not a booking agency, though we do coordinate the calendars for some of us. We're not a big studio, though we have a nice, comfy 24-track digital (Yay for ADAT!) place that's seen plenty of action. We're not a band, though we play a lot together. It's a scene. We're a Family. We hang out. When we encounter a challenge, it's not in the virtual realm, it's for real. There's no Restart button anywhere. We just have to deal with it. *How* I deal with it (with the CrossWalk mentees watching) is the mentoring process. That's how Jesus did it.

Sometimes they watch me succeed, and they learn. Other times they see me fail, and they learn. Sometimes I'm so good, I'm floating. Sometimes I'm drowning. But, hey, this is the deep end. And when the day is done, I can always go home and listen to Ray sing. That's how Van did it.

Clouds of Witness

My Dad spent his early years in the stately but austere Orphan House in Charleston, South Carolina. In his teens, he worked at the Naval ship yard there and, like the prodigal son, spent his life in "riotous living." But after a World War II stint in the Army Air Corps as a flight engineer, God got hold of my Dad. He felt a call into the ministry and spent the rest of his life touching those who, like him, had no place to call home but the House of God.

I remember falling asleep on the front pew as he preached in the churches he'd planted in rural Georgia. I remember potlucks after church under the shade of pine trees, eating fried chicken, black-eyed peas and watermelon and drinking sweet tea. Later, we traveled the world as he served as a chaplain in the Air Force. In his retirement years, he and my mom made many missionary trips around the world and touched the lives of thousands of people.

My Dad died unexpectedly on July 13, 1991. Of course, we all miss him. But we believe in the resurrection and in heaven. He has joined the "cloud of witnesses" written about in Hebrews.

I like that biblical metaphor because I have a frequently recurring image that crosses my mind when I am in concert. Sometimes I will back away from the microphone after a song and, while the audience applauds, I'll "see" my Dad in the cloud of witnesses, cheering me on. It gives me a great deal of encouragement to think that he has preceded me and is applauding my efforts.

But the question I ask myself is this: What have I done that is worthy of applause in heaven? Maybe they like my songs. Maybe they laugh at my anecdotes. Maybe they are moved by my stories. I don't know, maybe all of the above. And maybe none of the above.

Perhaps what moves them are things I overlook or can't see—the kind word spoken to the exasperated flight attendant, the simple and sincere prayer offered before the concert by a young volunteer, the sudden burst of spiritual illumination that comes to someone as they finally realize and experience the depth of the love God has for them, the hug a child gives me after the concert is over and everyone is going home.

What gets a rousing response in heaven? What makes the cloud of witnesses rise up with a shout of joy? We who trust in Jesus and lay our hope in the resurrection also believe this: that there is a great difference between the value systems of heaven and earth. Sometimes we count our successes in numbers of people at our concerts, or numbers of units sold of our recordings, or dollars earned, or articles written, or awards received or applause given. However, maybe a more vital question is this: Is the cloud of witnesses cheering us on in these things or are they waiting for something else? Perhaps lots of something else—the character of Christ growing in us, the pursuit of holiness, the giving of care to "the least of these," the sacrifice of praise, the commitment to God and God alone...and you can add to this list yourself.

Jesus said that we would be judged by every idle word we speak. Did He speak that as a threat, or as a reminder to us to see each word as possibly an eternally damning indictment? Or could He have meant simply that our character slips out in the unguarded moments and the unplanned actions, in the words that we don't premeditate? Could it be that what we do "for show"—and what is often loudly cheered by earthly onlookers—is dismissed in heaven in favor of the smaller, private expressions of His love. Tell me, what part of my life gets the best response from my Dad and the rest of the cloud of witnesses...and from Jesus?

I visited Mother Teresa's Home for the Destitute and Dying in Calcutta, India, on two occasions. Each time, I was impressed with the tender love the staff showed to the dying beggars that lay gaunt and passive on the rows of beds. I sat on the edge of a bed and sang to forty abandoned boys in the Calcutta Mission of Mercy Boys' Home. I thought about my Dad at their age in the Charleston Orphan House. I could "see" him in the clouds of witness. And, while those boys and I laughed and sang, I think I heard him cheering me on.

Author Listing

Leann Albrecht
P.O. Box 1533
Goodlettsville TN 37070
Phone/Fax: 615-851-5877
E-mail: lmalbrecht@aol.com

Dave Michael Bell
Dancing Heart Music
8635 Callaghan Road
San Antonio TX 78230
Phone: 210-349-2295
Fax: 210-341-7547
E-mail: davemichael
    @dancingheart.com
Web:
    www.dancingheart.com

Kim Bollinger
11701 Rossmoor
St. Louis MO 63128
Phone: 314-843-7184
E-mail: bollinger@
    freewwweb.com

Steve Bowersox
Bowersox Institute of Music
3447 Heron Drive N.
Jacksonville FL 32250
Phone: 904-246-8248

Scott Wesley Brown
International Christian
    Artists Reaching the Earth
2151 Hartland Drive
Franklin TN 37069
Phone/Fax: 615-595-8180
E-mail: swbicare@aol.com
Web: www.community-web.
    com/icare/

Terry Butler
c/o Vineyard Music Group
5300 E. La Palma Avenue
Anaheim CA 92807
E-mail: vmgusa@vmg.com

John Chevalier
Moriah Ministries
7850 N. Silverbell —
    Suite 114-153
Tucson AZ 85743
Phone: 800-239-5719
E-mail: JohnChev05@
    aol.com

Phil Christensen
P.O. Box 100
Brightwood OR 97011
Voice mail: 503-499-7549
E-mail: indiecentral@
    juno.com

Curt Coffield
Resurrection Life Church
5100 Ivanrest Ave. SW
Grandville MI 49418
Phone: 616-534-4923
Fax: 616-534-6361

Steve Cook
PDI Ministries
7881 Beechcraft Avenue
    — Suite B
Gaithersburg MD 20879
Phone: 800-736-2202
Web: www.pdinet.org

Lindell Cooley
Music Missions International
P.O. Box 9788
Pensacola FL 32513
Phone: 850-455-2110
Fax: 850-455-3133
Web: www.mmi-inc.com

Tommy Coomes
P.O. Box 28807
Santa Ana CA 92799-8807
Phone: 714-557-6339
Fax: 714-557-6367
E-mail: coomsie@aol.com

Kirk and Deby Dearman
Christ Episcopal
115 Conception Street
Mobile AL 36602
Phone: 334-438-1822
Fax: 334-433-1854
E-mail: ChristEpch@aol.com

Daniel Douma
3201 Briarcliff Ave.
Ft. Smith AR 72908-8301
Phone: 501-648-3910

Byron Easterling
4455 Camp Bowie —
    Suite 214
Ft. Worth TX 76107
Phone: 817-731-7755

Beth Emery-Bryant
15613 Dorset Road #101
Laurel, MD 20707
Phone: 301-498-8405
Immanuel's Church
Phone: 301-989-4673

Darrell Evans
River Flow Ministries
334-639-2291

Chris Falson
Web: www.chrisfalson.com

David Fischer
Living Waters Christian
  Fellowship
2495 E. Mountain
Pasadena CA 91104
Phone: 626-791-7295
Fax: 626-791-7634
E-mail: FischLine@aol.com

Rick Founds
The Comfort Zone Ministries
26895 Aliso Creek Road
Box 419
Aliso Viejo CA 92656
Phone: 949-360-9320
Fax: 949-362-9905
E-mail: rickfounds@
  prtcl.com

Robert Gay
Prophetic Praise Ministries
P.O. Box 966
Lynn Haven FL 32444
Phone: 850-874-9743
Fax: 850-874-9744

Doug Hanks
P.O. Box 1016
Claremont CA 91711-1016
Phone: 909-625-2029
E-mail: doughanks@
  earthlink.net

Frank Hernandez
HeartChild Ministries
1120 Blue Springs Road
Franklin TN 37069-6937
Phone: 615-377-1199
E-mail: heartchld@aol.com

Daniel Jacobi
Dr-Heinrich-Jasper-Str. 20
37581 Bad Gandersheim
GERMANY
Phone: 011-49-5382-930174
Fax: 011-49-5382-930100
E-mail: Jacobi.Daniel@
  t-online.de

Brad Kauffman
The Church of Grace
  and Peace
2 Rt. 37 West
Toms River NJ 08753
Phone: 732-349-1550
Fax: 732-286-6311
E-mail: brad.kauffman@
  usa.net
Web: www.graceandpeace
  .org

Monty Kelso
Director of Creative
  Communication
Coast Hills Community Ch.
#5 Pursuit
Aliso Viejo CA 92656
Phone: 949-362-0079
E-mail: mkelso@
  coasthillschurch.org

Bob Kilpatrick
P.O. Box 2383
Fair Oaks CA 95628
Phone: 916-961-1022

Tom Kraeuter
Training Resources, Inc.
8929 Old LeMay Ferry Rd
Hillsboro MO 63050
Phone/Fax: 314-789-4522
E-mail: KraeuterT@aol.com

Karen Lafferty
Musicians for Missions Int'l
YWAM Santa Fe
P.O. Box 22009
Sante Fe NM 87502
Phone/Fax: 505-471-5872
E-mail: MFMI_KL@
  compuserve.com

Bruce Harry Larson
First Assembly of God
3401 19th St South
Fargo ND 58104
Phone: 701-232-0003
Fax: 701-280-2410
E-mail: BHLarson@
  juno.com

Charlie and Jill LeBlanc
Joyful Word Ministries, Inc.
P.O. Box 4396
Chesterfield MO 63006-4396
Phone: 314-530-9690
Fax: 314-530-9078
E-mail: JWMCJ@aol.com

Sally Morgenthaler
Worship Evangelism
  Concepts
salmorgen@aol.com

Rob Packer
Life Way Ministries
P.O. Box 303
Warkworth 1241, Auckland
NEW ZEALAND
Phone: 011-64-9-425-4054
Fax: 011-64-9-425-4053
E-mail: rpacker@
   voyager.co.nz

Andy Park
North Langley Vineyard
9089 Glover Road
Fort Langley BC V1M 2S1
CANADA
Fax: 604-513-8463

Steve Phifer
Suncoast Cathedral
2300 62 Ave N
St Petersburg FL 33702
Phone: 813-522-2171
Fax: 813-525-4673

Bill Rayborn
TCMR Communications, Inc.
P.O. Box 1179
Grapevine TX 76099-1179
Phone: 817-488-0141
Fax: 817-481-4191
E-mail: tcmrtalk@airmail.net
Web: www.tcmr.com

Robb Redman
Worship Min. Resources Ctr.
252 Wyanoke Dr.
San Antonio TX 78209
Phone: 210-804-0061
Fax: 210-804-0190
E-mail: wmrc@
   worshipministry.com
Web: www.worshipministry
   .com

Randy Rothwell
10203 Champions Circle
Franklin TN 37064
Phone: 615-595-2633
Fax: 615-794-6248
E-mail: ranman@nc5.infi.net

Gary Sadler
1397 Hunter Rd
Franklin TN 37064
Phone/Fax: 615-794-5214
E-mail: gesad@aol.com

Gary Shelton
Skywork Ministries
5541 Oakville Center #107
Phone: 314-846-1945
Fax: 314-846-2238
E-mail: Skywrok1@aol.com
Web: www.grmi.org/
   ministry/skywork

Scott Smith
Bethel Temple Assembly
1705 Todds Lane
Hampton VA 23666
Phone: 757-826-1426
Fax: 757-826-5436
E-mail: BethelTemple@
   juno.com

Bob Sorge
Oasis House
P.O. Box 957
Canandaigua NY 14424
Phone: 716-394-4640
Fax: 394-7027

The Rev. Dr. John R. Throop
The Summit Group
P.O. Box 3794
Peoria IL 61612-3794
Phone: 309-681-1118 (cont'd)

Fax: 309-681-1137
E-mail: jthroop@
   concentric.net

Geoff Thurman
HAVuHEARD? Ministries
JuWanFryzWiDat? Music
1625 Sulphur Springs Road
Murfreesboro TN 37129
Phone: 615-895-1131

Tommy Walker
Get Down Records
2424 Colorado
Los Angeles CA 90041
Phone: 213-255-8016
E-mail: getdown@
   primenet.com
Web: www.getdownrecords
   .com

Cheri Walters
Canyon Country Assembly
27053 Honby Avenue
Canyon Country CA 91351
Phone: 805-251-2770
E-mail: c_walters@
   hotmail.com

Kelly Willard
P.O. Box 2222
Lebanon TN 37088
Phone: 615-449-0339
E-mail: willinghart@aol.com

Darlene Zschech
Hills Christian Life Centre
P.O. Box 1195
Castle Hill NSW 1765
AUSTRALIA
Fax: 011-612-9899-4591

ORDER FORM

	QTY	EACH	TOTAL
Worship Is...What?!		$ 8.00	
If Standing Together Is So Great, Why Do We Keep Falling Apart?		$ 8.00	
Things They Didn't Teach Me In Worship Leading School		$10.00	
Keys to Becoming an Effective Worship Leader		$ 8.00	
Developing an Effective Worship Ministry		$ 8.00	
The Worship Leader's Handbook		$ 9.00	
		Subtotal	

Postage/Packaging — 10% of subtotal for U.S. & Canada, minimum $1.50; 40% for overseas

TOTAL

☐ Enclosed is my check for $_____
   made payable to EMERALD BOOKS

PAYMENT OPTIONS

☐ Credit Card — Please bill my:

☐ MC ☐ Visa   Credit Card Exp._____

Card#_____

Signature_____

Name_____

_____

Address_____

City_____ ST_____ ZIP_____

Phone_____ E-mail_____

Mail to: Training Resources • 8929 Old LeMay Ferry Rd. • Hillsboro, MO 63050

Please allow 2-3 weeks for delivery

Telephone orders (charge cards only) call: (636) 789-4522.
Monday through Friday, 9:00 - 4:00 CST